Eyes
on the
Cross

April 4

Eyes on the Cross

A Guide for Contemplation

Michael Kennedy, S.J.

Illustrations by
Bernardo Gantier Zelada, S.J.

Christian Application
project 1970
at the camp
grounds
in Kentucky

Jim Moore

A Crossroad Book
The Crossroad Publishing Company
New York

Scripture citations are taken from *Christian Community Bible: Catholic Pastoral Edition*, 14th ed., copyright © 1994 by Bernardo Hurault, used with the permission of Claretian Publications, U.P. P.O. Box 4, Quezon City 1101, Philippines.

The Crossroad Publishing Company
481 Eighth Avenue, New York, NY 10001

Printed in the United States of America

Library of Congress Cataloging-in-Publication Data

Kennedy, Michael, S.J.
    Eyes on the Cross / Michael Kennedy ; illustrations by
    Bernardo Gantier Zelada.
        p.   cm.
    Includes bibliographical references.
    ISBN 0-8245-1879-9 (alk. paper)
    1. Jesus Christ – Biography – Meditations. 2. Bible. N.T.
    Gospels – Meditations. 3. Contemplation. 4. Spiritual exercises.
    I. Title.
    BT306.4 .K48 2000
    232.9'01 – dc21

                                                    00-010136

1 2 3 4 5 6 7 8 9 10   06 05 04 03 02 01 00

Contents

Contents

foreword

What does it mean to have hope, especially in the midst of suffering and abandonment? This is a question most of us have faced at one time or another. Usually it arises unexpectedly, in events or circumstances mostly beyond our control: the loss of a child, divorce, the experience of exile, debilitating depression, chronic illness, or any number of nameless fears and anxieties that keep us awake at night. Is God with us in these moments? Does God journey with us, even sustain us in those moments when the very bottom seems to have dropped out of our lives? Or have we been left to fend for ourselves? Are our lives without pattern, without meaning?

I consider these questions as I look at the small group of young men sitting before me in Central Juvenile Hall in Los Angeles. We have gathered in a cramped room on the second floor of the M and N unit. The boys wear bright orange, signifying their classification as high-risk offenders. From the main room just beyond the door I can hear shouts: the other boys in the unit are finishing their showers, preparing for dinner. In here it is quiet. The boys exchange shy greetings with Mike Kennedy and me. We take a few moments to check in, to see how everyone is doing. They seem glad to be here, glad for the chance to be in this place apart for a few minutes. We are all glad to be here. Gradually we settle into a quieter space. A candle is lit. Music plays softly. We are invited to enter into prayer, bowing our heads as Mike slowly reads the meditation. This afternoon it is "Beneath the Cross."

We allow ourselves to be drawn into that terrible place, pause for a moment in the presence of Mary, listen to her bewilderment:

> looking at my son
> feeling the suffering...
> i wish i could put myself
> in your place
> but i can't

There is a deep stillness in the room now. The boys' heads are bowed low, as though they were listening very carefully, trying to pick up something deep within the words. What is it? Then I realize: every boy in this room has heard his own mother say these words, or words very close to these. When they were arrested. Or standing before a judge in a courtroom. Or perhaps on Sundays (the only day of the week in which the boys can see their mothers). Their mothers. They are thinking about, feeling the presence of their mothers.

In this moment, perhaps more clearly than ever before for some of the boys, they are coming to see the depth and steadfastness of their mothers' love for them; they are feeling the immensity of the suffering they have caused their mothers; and they are opening themselves to the aching sadness they feel at having to live at such a distance from their mothers.

In the process, they are being drawn near to God. I am guessing at most of this as it is happening. I don't know for certain what the boys are thinking about. But I can sense how deeply the words of the meditation move them.

Perhaps it is because I myself have been drawn so deeply into this place of desolation at the foot of the cross, because of the associations and feelings I am having about my own mother. Later they will write and speak of these things, of their feelings of loss, sadness, and grief. They will express their sense of anguish and guilt over what they have done, especially the guilt they feel at having let down their mothers. And they will describe the changes that have begun to take hold within them, the new vision of their own lives that has begun to emerge, the sense of hope they are beginning to feel. Objectively, there is not much to feel hopeful about. Some of these boys are facing serious prison time. Some will be old before they taste freedom. Some will never walk free again. Yet, somehow an authentic sense of hope seems to be taking deep root in them.

I am sure it has something to do with what happens in these meditations. No one is preaching at them. No one is attempting to "teach" them anything. They are being invited to use their imaginations and their senses to enter into the space of the Gospels, to let themselves feel with every fiber of their being the healing, transforming power of Jesus. They are being invited to draw near to Jesus, close enough to touch and be held by him, close enough to hear his words addressed directly to them. Here is a climate of intimacy, forgiveness, and love. Not as a mere idea, but as a palpable reality.

Still, love cannot enter in where there is no risk. That is the only requirement for entering into the space of these meditations. Risk. A commitment to honest engagement with oneself, others, and God. This is something I notice about these boys: because they have lost so much already,

because they have seen their illusions of self-sufficiency
and invulnerability stripped away so completely, they are
willing to risk themselves deeply. They are willing to stand
before God in their nakedness, in their helplessness, in
their need.

This is a place we are all invited to stand — in that
place of risk where we can acknowledge our own deep
need and where we can enter into the lives of those others
in our midst who are lonely and bereft. Yet this is not
an easy place to be. We recoil from the call to practice
such demanding honesty and far-reaching compassion.
We would rather hide from ourselves and from those broken ones in our midst who call for our attention. Still, we
long for that call. We long to feel the touch of God in
the deepest part of our being. This, I believe, is why these
meditations are so compelling and so useful to us: they
reach into the very center of who we are and call forth
the hidden, the lost, the lonely one who dwells there, the
one who knows (even if that knowledge has been forgotten) that the love of God is the great truth at the center
of everything.

How can we learn to grasp this truth? How can we
open ourselves to a genuine encounter with the person
of Jesus, to a deep and abiding intimacy with God?
It requires a willingness to engage the whole self in
the quest for God — not only one's understanding but
also one's senses, one's imagination. This is the beauty
and power of the Ignatian tradition of meditation that
Michael Kennedy employs here to probe the Gospels:
through the senses and the imagination we are invited to
engage the whole reality of the Gospels — their words and
images as well as their fragrance and texture; the aching

sadness and emptiness that haunt the lives of so many who seek out the person of Jesus as well as the unexpected signs of grace and hope that emerge in the charged encounters they have with him.

To allow ourselves to be drawn in this close to Jesus is to open ourselves to profound risk; but it is also to open ourselves to the possibility of renewal and transformation. This is the allure and the terror involved in any genuine encounter with Jesus. Yet it requires imagination and courage to feel this terror and not turn away, to know this allure and allow it to stir and grow within us. This is precisely what is asked of the characters who encounter Jesus in the Gospels. It is also what is asked of each one of us.

Can we allow ourselves to sit with Peter beside the Sea of Galilee, listening to the "small breaking of waves / hitting the shore..." looking at "the moon reflecting / on the still surface / of the lake," asking ourselves — honestly — in the face of Jesus' mesmerizing presence: "What do I desire?" Can we acknowledge, with Sarah, our sickness, our tremendous need? Can we open ourselves as she did to receive the "fragrant oil...to rub the oil / against the palms / of [our] hands / then smell the oil / then put our hands / against our hearts" and be healed? Are we willing to climb into the boat with Jesus and row out into the middle of the lake, to trust that lowering our nets into the deep waters will yield the fruit we are seeking? Can we muster the courage to walk with Jesus into that place of blood and brokenness and abandonment, the place of the cross, to enter into and not flee from the places of suffering into which we ourselves are called to enter? This is the great work we are invited to engage in here,

the work of facing and struggling with these fundamental
questions of faith, of entering into those places — of joy
and abandonment — where faith and hope are born.

There is no doubt a solitary dimension to such work.
But at its heart it is a fundamentally communal work.
It would be difficult to read these meditations and not
notice how profoundly they arise from within a lived
experience of Christian community. It is not an ideal community. Indeed, many of those whose presence can be felt
both directly and indirectly in the pages of this book must
be counted as among the most broken and bereft among
us. Some of them, barely more than children, are prison-
ers, young men and women whose lives on the streets of
East Los Angeles amid poverty, gangs, crime, and violence
have landed them in a place of bleak sadness. Others are
immigrants, drawn to this country because of war and
violence in their homelands or in the hopes of finding
work and a fuller, more secure life for themselves and
their families; theirs is often a precarious, lonely existence.
And there are a host of others — the author himself, a
Jesuit priest with a longstanding commitment to the struggle against injustice, parishioners from Dolores Mission
Church in East Los Angeles, children from the local parish school, associate pastoral ministers, fellow Jesuits —
whose presence can also be felt in these meditations.

Much of the hope to be derived from this book — and
it is a strong and deep hope, I believe — derives from
the honesty and courage arising from the midst of this
remarkable community. It is a community engaged in a
struggle common to us all: the struggle to embrace our
fragile humanity, to find sources of hope arising from the
ambiguous, often painful, circumstances of our lives, and

to help bring into concrete reality the elusive but ever present kingdom of God. It is the struggle of Jesus, the struggle of the Gospels.

To pick up and read these meditations, then, is to find ourselves called to enter more and more deeply into those places — in the world, in the church, and in our own lives — where hope seems most elusive. Here are stories and images that can help give us the courage to enter those places and dwell there, to struggle with our own deepest fears and perhaps carry for a while some of the broken ones we find there. To keep our eyes on the cross and not turn away is the most painful and demanding of challenges. Yet without such faithful attention to the cross, to the broken and abandoned ones in our midst, is hope really possible?

DOUGLAS BURTON-CHRISTIE

dedication

When I was first ordained, I worked at a parish in San Diego. Kenny, a member of our parish youth group, was one of those kids from the inner city who was going to make it. He had just received a full four-year scholarship to a good university. One Thursday morning, two days before graduation, Kenny drowned at his senior outing. I still remember embracing Kenny's mother, Brenda, at the hospital. Her outcry of grief filled the entire hospital. I recall listening to that wailing, thinking, "I don't know what I would do with the agony of the loss of a child." This deep expression of grief still haunts me after twenty years.

I remember, one night at a liturgy in El Salvador, speaking with a group of mothers who had all recently lost sons in the war. María with a pained face, terribly wrinkled and weather worn, expressed her grief softly, speaking of how all her five sons where killed on the same night one month ago. I also remember Isabel, who after losing her husband to the war, endured the loss of her son, José, who stepped on a mine in his repatriated village. José died in the hospital. How do you continue after such intense loss?

More recently, I felt the anguish of Virginia as the judge read at the sentencing of her son, "Mario R. to serve twenty-nine years to life plus a second life term that will be served consecutively." The outburst of anguish in that courtroom reminded me of Brenda's, María's, Isabel's, and other countless parents' cries of loss.

During these last years, I have on a regular basis sat around a table sharing a meal and listening to parents talk about the loss, the pain of having the ones they have given life to now incarcerated for many years to come. I have felt many times how profound and deep is a parents' love. The parents whose sons are in prison have taught me many things in their willingness to share, to comfort, and to support each other.

I know it is possible to endure and pass only through this pain with the help of One greater and with the help of each other. Somehow, I always leave these encounters with a small vestige of hope that, in spite of everything, it is worthwhile struggling and loving. I dedicate this book to all these parents who have endured deep loss:

Brenda, María, Isabel, Camilla, Vikki,
Lety, Martín, Virginia, Irma, Lucía, María,
Irma, Marta, Darío, Francisco, Isidra, Lupe,
Alicia, Cándida, Margarita, Aurora, Eduvelia

acknowledgments

I walked through the entrance of Central Juvenile Hall. As I neared one of the units, José knocked on the tinted window, holding up *Eyes on Jesus,* my first book published by Crossroad. I felt good to know that someone experiencing tremendous distress and fear could find meaning in developing his inner life. I am grateful to Gwendolin, Paul, Christine, John, Alison, and Althea of Crossroad Publishing Company. Your confidence in me and your careful work in publishing this book makes it possible for me to share the gift of hope that I have received from the many with whom I have journeyed through grief and joy, through death and resurrection.

I would also like to thank Mary Ellen and Doug Burton-Christie, who were always there to encourage and help in the process of writing this book. They were totally amazing.

I am grateful to Dick Howard, Eddy Martínez, Hector Gonzales, Gabrielle Porter, and Mike Roide, who helped with the many and assorted technical details in this adventure.

I am also grateful to my Jesuit brothers of Casa Espinal: Robert Dolan, Greg Boyle, Ted Gabrielli, Mark Torres, John Lipson, Bill Cain, Elias Puentes, Chris Donahue, Mike Eng, Greg Caumann, and Greg Bonfiglio, who along with the staff and community of Dolores Mission Parish have inspired me to continue working to make this a better world.

introduction

Toni schedules retreats at Serra Retreat House in Malibu. This year we had our eighth grade retreat at the same time as a workshop for new pastors. I thought to myself, "This could be a real disaster, eighth graders and new pastors." I saw Toni at lunch and said, "I hope the kids were all right." She then told me not only how well behaved they were but also how impressed she was with the prayerfulness of these kids, how seriously they took prayer. This woke me up. Perhaps I had felt too close to the experience of working with these kids with contemplation, to see this concrete result but when Toni told me this, it helped me to see what really was before me.

On that retreat day at Malibu, from nine to twelve in the morning, we used three meditations contained in this book. Every Friday for a year, these eighth graders had gone up to the third floor of our parish school, where we have created a meditation chapel. They learned to go inward, to be silent, not to be afraid of what surfaces. They have learned the discipline of reflecting on their experience and then writing about it. This retreat was a culmination of a year's practice. After Toni made the comment, I thought to myself, "Mike, you should feel good about these great barrio kids and the experience they are having on this retreat. This year-long discipline of contemplation has paid off."

I have always thought that together with the "head" knowledge of our faith, an experience of who Jesus is can have lasting effects in people's lives. This group of twenty-five eighth graders reaffirmed this belief. To develop a contemplative attitude is difficult for any of us. I hope that these eighth graders will continue what they began this past year. As they graduate they will take with them the experience that their religion is not just about attending to external obligations but is also about developing an inner life, a relationship with Jesus that can have lasting and important consequences for the rest of their lives.

One of the most powerful experiences of using these contemplations happened in preparation for Holy Week at Central Juvenile Hall. The beautiful sunny day outside contrasted with the dark, damp hallways that one experiences in the girls' Unit AB of Central Juvenile Hall. I soon found myself in a large dormitory with Javier, the chaplain of the detention center where over a thousand youth are incarcerated. Antoinette came in first. She is a beautiful seventeen-year-old African American girl with a strong presence about her. After listening to what she read that afternoon, I reflected that if Antoinette were not wearing the orange suit of a high-risk youth, she could be an English major at UCLA.

Antoinette had written some reflections on the Stations of the Cross that we were going to use two days later for our Good Friday service. She read her first reflection about Jesus being condemned to death. She compared it to her life in Central Juvenile Hall and added, "What is so unfair about us being locked up is that some of us maybe have messed up and done something bad, but we are not criminals. We are not given a second chance. In many ways we are still kids." After she finished reading, she asked us if we were going to bring chocolate Easter eggs on Sunday.

Slowly the other girls filed into the room: Laura, Alexandra, Helen, Kimberly, and Ruby. Javier explained that this was Holy Week and we were going to pray about the cross, but that we were going to do it in a special manner today. We were going to use a way that is very old and is connected to a saint named Ignatius of Loyola. Javier explained that contemplation is one of among many ways of praying. He told the girls that even though they cannot physically leave this building, they can travel to other places by means of their imagination. The method we were going to use can make the Gospel passage real, as if we were actually present, taking part in the scene. He finished the explanation by saying how this same method is the one we use every week in the boys' unit and also during liturgies on Sundays.

"Today we will pray on the cross and how it is connected to our lives," Javier began. "We will then answer one question at the end of the contemplation: What one person in our life has been there for us like Mary was there for Jesus beneath the cross?" We put the music on, lit the candle, and then I explained how after the meditation I would anoint their hands. They would be invited to rub their hands together with this special oil, smell it, and then place it against their hearts.

Javier began to read the meditation:

> wondering
> when this would ever end
> or would it ever end
> wanted to escape somehow

run away from this spot
felt so weak
so vulnerable
tried to utter a prayer
recite some scripture
i had learned
when i was a small girl
but nothing came to me
as i stood beneath the cross

Holy Week in itself has such power. But sitting in that
room listening to this story, being with these six young
women, created an experience that truly allowed us to
transcend the bars, the stale smells and the loud noises
in the hallways. We were able to travel back through time
to a certain hill where a mother stood with her "criminal"
son. Javier continued to read slowly:

i am glad
i have been your mother
you have been the best son
imaginable
even though at times
i did not understand
what you were saying
or what you were doing
i see now
that your way
is god's way

When he finished, we briefly remained in silence. Then
I went around this circle of prayer, rubbing the oil into
their hands in the form of a cross. They rubbed it

against their hands, smelled it, and placed their hands against their hearts. Something powerful was happening in that room.

The girls then took up their pens and began to write their reflections. They wrote how Mary was there for Jesus and how their moms were there for them. After finishing, each girl took the candle and began to read about the moving ways in which their mothers had stood by them in the worst times. The tenderness and love that flowed was interrupted only by tears. That afternoon these girls were very vulnerable to each other. In that dormitory room there was nowhere to hide like there was on the streets. I also was moved to tears listening to them talk about the presence of their mothers for them.

Antoinette reflected, "It took me so long to be able to say these words that I'm about to say, and, man, I mean it with all my heart: Mom, I apologize for everything that I have done to hurt you." Helen stated, "I know you're upset that I'm in jail and not right there with you like I'm supposed to be. But you still love me, and that's all I need from you." And Alexandra added, "I hate to see you go home after those visits that never seem long enough. My words can't explain the pain I feel inside right now. I need your warm, tender embrace."

We finished the meditation by holding hands and each one named her mother and prayed for her. We blew out the candle. I felt that we were slowly coming out of a dream, an experience that was able to take us far away from being incarcerated. It was so connected to what Holy Week is about: how on the cross, where we least expect to find God, Jesus manifested who God really is. The very darkest place contained the brightest light.

After I blew out the candle, we exchanged the sign of peace. The tenderness with which these girls gave each other peace, how they embraced each other, was the final touch of the deep experience of light in this place of darkness. On one level, the care they were expressing for each other was connected to memories of how their mothers have stood by them. On another level, somehow our crucified God was mixed up in these embraces. God was letting them feel that the Crucified One also cares about them, accepts them, and loves them so much that Jesus was also somehow lovingly embracing each girl. God was letting them feel the raw mystery of this week, which can be experienced only in the darkest places, where there is nothing else except the cross revealing the insides of God. I think we could have stayed all night in this circular embrace.

When Javier and I walked out of Juvenile Hall, I felt as if I were coming out of a deep experience and now had to reenter ordinary time. I only wish that those who pass such harsh laws to deal with juveniles could have been there.

The contemplations that are found in this book have been used in many different settings during this past year. They can be used either privately or in groups. There are questions at the end of each chapter that can be used to open up some thoughts after the meditation. For some people it helps to write after the contemplation and then to share these reflections in a group. What is important is to begin to take seriously our own religious experience. Jesus becomes more real. For some, the contemplations have been a valuable way to discern, to make a good decision.

These contemplations have been used with Antoinette, with people like Paul, a lawyer, with Dante, an accountant, with Eric from Loyola Marymount University and Javier the student body president of Santa Clara University. In some small way, each of these people is learning not only to take on more of the mind of Jesus, but by seeing, feeling, and experiencing Jesus in the contemplations, they are all learning to pay attention to the movements of the Spirit within them. People are hungry for religious experience. What happened to those eighth graders at Malibu or to those girls in Juvenile Hall manifests how God is very much alive and interacting with us.

I would like to suggest a few ways in which this book can be used when it is not used in a group, ways that have been drawn from the fruit of my own and others' experience:

1. Find a comfortable and quiet place. Close your eyes, relax, leave concerns in God's care while you pray. Quietly remember that God is now with you and welcoming your full attention.

2. Slowly read the passage from the Gospel.

3. Allow yourself to become absorbed in what is taking place in the scene. How is each person feeling and what is each person doing? How am I feeling and what am I doing?

4. Now slowly read over the corresponding contemplation from this book. Use the contemplation like a springboard to enter more deeply and completely into the scene.

5. Use your senses. Taste, touch, feel, smell, and see what is going on around you. Express yourself in the scene. Talk with those present. Become part of the scene itself.

6. Let God do the rest. Whatever thoughts, feelings, and body sensations come, let them flow freely and allow them to deepen your contact with God. Often God reveals things to us that we could never have imagined or arrived at through merely "thinking" about them.

friendship

john 1:35–39

It is summer and our parish team is at the Serra Retreat House in Malibu making our retreat together. The chapel is dark. You can no longer see the sparkling blue ocean. Earlier in the afternoon, we had written about what we were most grateful for with regard to each member of our pastoral team of the parish. It is now 9:00 p.m. It is time to read what each person has written. The flickering from the candles is lighting up each face.

In 1984, Arturo had started working at Casa Grande, a refugee house at Blessed Sacrament Parish in Hollywood for Salvadorans and Guatemalans fleeing persecution. I read some very simple words of how his commitment to immigrants reflected Jesus' own compassion. In the year 2000, Arturo is still working with immigrants, now at Dolores Mission Church. Still with the same zeal and sensitivity.

Around that altar, sitting with friends, I was feeling the bonds of friendship, having worked together to build a better world. I could almost see, feel in the eyes of Arturo the children who were maimed by mines in El Salvador and who had spent one Christmas at Casa Grande in 1987. Images of Francisco, who had stepped on a mine, hobbling up and down the stairs. God could be touched

27

in the exchanges of those Christmas days with children whose bodies bore the marks of a bloody war.

Now in the chapel, sitting around that circle, I feel how important it is to grow in friendship with Jesus, giving us strength to continue, not for one year, not for two, but for life. This night in the chapel at Malibu, feeling the bonds of friendship flow between us, I am grateful for both the One who called us to enter into such a commitment and grateful for those with whom I am working.

On the following day John was standing there again with two of his disciples. As Jesus walked by, John looked at him and said, "There is the Lamb of God." On hearing this, the two disciples followed Jesus. He turned and saw them following, and he said to them, "What are you looking for?" They answered, "Rabbi (which means Master), where are you staying?" Jesus said, "Come and see." So they went and saw where he stayed and spent the rest of that day with him. It was about four o'clock in the afternoon.

> no clouds
> only long endless blue
> walking this afternoon
> along the bank
> of the river
> walking with the baptist
> watching the currents
> of the river
> wash over rocks

deep at some places
the baptist saying
there he is
walking
under the shade
of the tree
go
you will learn
much from him
many thoughts
flowed through me
stronger
than the water flowing
trying to keep up
with him
as he became lost
again and again
in the shade
andrew
telling me
that we should
hurry up
and tell him
that the baptist sent us
but something
within me
wanted to follow him longer
walking
watching
as he gazed
at all the people
gathering

to seek to enter the water
watching as he stopped
spoke
with the children
with their parents
　it was an ordinary afternoon
　had risen early
　long before the sun
　in order
　to be at the river
　before the crowds arrived
thinking of all the events
of past days
the faces and faces
of those speaking
of their desire
to change
to be lost
in the water
my own life had changed
so much
since i helped the baptist
the one in front of us
suddenly turning
down where trees meet
to move away
from the sound
of the river flowing
away from the noise
of so many desiring
strongly to enter water
why were we following him?

at least
will go a little further
slowly ascending incline
just as i was pondering
how we were going
to meet him
he turns toward us
at the place
where the path
is lost in the hills
no longer
with a view of river
peering as we continue
to walk
closer to where
he is standing
so the baptist
wants us to meet
this one now close
now no longer
safe distance
between us
hearing
can i help you?
are you looking
for someone?
opening my mouth
we watched you
as you walked
along the river
looking at him
still with no name

what are we looking for?
a thousand cords of tangled nets
broke loose in my heart
feeling the memories
from my youth
memories
   of the restlessness
   i have felt
   restlessness
   about something
   was wrong
   with the degree
   of suffering
   our people have to endure
now this one
who mirrored the flowing
of the river
suddenly lost in the moment
his presence pulled me deep
into the deepest place
of the river flowing
what do i desire?
remember
first time i walked into
the synagogue at capernaum
i was pulled deep into presence
same presence
feeling now
creating deep space
desiring to be filled
even after all these years
have not forgotten that experience

but how do i put words
for a yearning
as wide as the endless
stretch of blue sky?
i wanted to tell
this stranger all this
but stumbled out
where do you live?
how could i say that?
what a stupid thing to say
where do you live?
but he seemed pleased
by this question
his eyes lit up
my name is jesus
i am staying close
i have been alone
for many days now
i would like you
to accompany me
would like you to walk
with me
we can talk
as we journey
to my dwelling
this was the moment
connecting to the first time
i walked into the synagogue
to the moments
to the times
when i would get up early
to fish

and would stare up
at the darkened sky
with bright stars
a stillness
at this time of day
falling deep into the presence
this one called jesus
evoked same feeling
knew i needed
to say yes
needed to follow
this deep yearning
connected
to something
to someone more
in this universe
that i never found
in our religious leaders
so preoccupied
about possessions
yes master jesus
i would like to see
where you live
would like to join you
slowly we left that spot
but knew
   in that deep space
   below the river
   same place
   where i fell into many years ago
   felt right speaking with this one
walking

speaking of our deep desires
didn't want this journeying
to end
quickly we covered the distance
to jesus' dwelling
hidden between trees
opening door
inviting us to enter
his house
as i passed into the darkened space
  i even fell deeper
  connecting
  to thoughts
  i had many times
  when i pondered
  what was the moment like
  passing out of this world
  into the next
  what happens?
  where do you go?
  where is your house then?
  where do you dwell?
  but in this lost moment
  passing through this door
  i experienced
  a feeling of belonging
  i had never felt
  in my life
  i knew
  what was happening
  within
i would never forget that place

where i felt deep presence
wasn't sure
what to say
   but jesus
   began to talk
about his time apart
   how he saw everything different
   he would now like
   to see how conditions
   could be changed
   for the excluded
   of society
this gave me confidence
to tell jesus
how my relatives
were taken off their land
because the taxes were so overbearing
i started to be moved
   telling jesus
   the sorrow i felt
   seeing so much suffering
   in our land
   so much injustice
   as we talked
   as we let
   the moment seize us
   knew jesus understood
   what i was saying
   he had lived it
   soon our conversation
   was flowing
   as quickly smoothly

as the river
we left behind
could feel as we walked
that the first bonds
of friendship
were being created

reflection questions

1. What would I say if Jesus were to turn and ask me, "What do you want?"

2. What do I yearn for? What does that yearning feel like? Can I say it in words?

3. Do I remember a time of feeling deeply connected to someone? In prayer? With a friend? What was that like?

cure of sarah

mark 1:29-31

It is Christmas time in the Lynwood Jail. I ask the group of forty men how many have children. Almost everyone does, and five of them have wives who are expecting to give birth soon. Two of them have six children. At the beginning of the meditation they are invited to picture their children, their wives, and enter into the contemplation, praying for a healing to take place on some level: to be healed from the loneliness of jail during this holiday season.

In the classroom/chapel I look into their faces. I can tell they are entering deeply into the experience. A stillness takes over. The One who never leaves us alone is very present. I put oil on their hands, they rub it, smell it, and put their hands against their hearts. This healing gesture breaks the stereotype of the macho inmate. There is a tenderness, a vulnerability that is palpable. Each one is invited to pray out loud the names of his wife and children. Suddenly the chapel seems full of laughing children and loving wives. God does not want us to be isolated, alone and separated. Never.

As soon as they left the synagogue, Jesus went to the home of Simon and Andrew with James and John. As

Simon's mother-in-law was sick in bed with fever, they immediately told him about her. Jesus went to her and taking her by the hand, raised her up. The fever left her and she began to wait on them.

was good making
this last stretch
before arriving at capernaum
ever since
i have walked with jesus
have wanted him
to meet my family
to see where my house is
my life had changed
so much
after joining jesus' group
during these last two months
the smells from the lake
were strong refreshing
as we descended
the last hill
before arriving at the gates
of the city
suddenly
in front of the deep blue
of the lake
wind strong
white crests covering the surface
talking to jesus
of life in this fishing village
i had learned
to fish before i could read

showed the group the synagogue
the school
felt good
to be showing
this part of my history
to my friends
finally nearing the shore
of the lake
approaching the door
of my house
when i left here
a few months ago
never imagined
i would be engaged
in this type of work
my family
had been fishermen
for years
whoever thought
i would be working
for a wandering preacher?

suddenly
surrounded by my family
introducing
my friends
i knew i needed to do
some explaining
but there was a look
of wide concern
on the face
of my wife

asking her
what was wrong
she started to cry
trying to say
her mother was terribly sick
she was afraid
she was going to die
could peter
ask his friend
the healer
to visit her
jesus saying
he would be glad to soon

kneeling down
beside the outstretched
almost lifeless body
of sarah
jesus looking at the sweat
at the paleness
of her skin
taking her hand
into his
how long
has she been like this?
you could tell
jesus did not like
what he saw
sarah's suffering intense

jesus
taking a small container
of rich oil

from his pocket
the smell from the oil
filled the whole room
cutting into the darkness
for one month
sarah had lain here
on this straw mat
with fever
with chills
not able to speak

jesus
putting a small amount
of fragrant oil
on her hands
her forehead
asking sarah
to rub the oil
against the palms
of her hands
then smell the oil
and then put her hands
against her heart

jesus
praying
feeling a powerful light
   abba
night and day
sarah suffers from this infirmity
   abba
   i rub
   this oil

rich in odor
against her hands
fragrant
let your healing touch
be felt
so she will not
be chained here
suffering
heal her
not just of this fever
but also whatever
causes darkness in her heart
the fear that encompasses her
since she does not
have the confidence
to share with her family
what happened
as jesus
rubbed
this scented oil
into her withered hand
the parts
that had been destroying her
were being touched
by the oil this oil
was absorbing the hurt
endured when her husband
had left her
as jesus rubbed the oil
on her other hand
the pain from her feelings
day after day

of having children
laugh at her
because of her severe limp
birth had delivered this defect
sometimes
life all seemed too unbearable

this warm scented oil
as jesus
rubbed it across her forehead
again and again
absorbed
all the memories
of when the romans
took away
her eldest son
she still remembers
every day
as her son
turned around
and looked at her
crying out for help
as a mother
she wanted to defend
her firstborn
that was the last time
she ever saw
her son
this pain
was being absorbed
by this oil
warm

being next to jesus
could feel
how jesus
was healing all the parts
of sarah
the fever the chills
were only signs
of the darkness
in her own heart
jesus
was bringing healing light
into her very center
this oil warm against
her flesh
absorbing the anger
sarah carried in her
against her neighbors
who would continuously
put her down
this healing oil
was absorbing
all this pent-up hurt
slowly this healing light
was absorbing
all the darkness
causing this fever
sarah
jesus said
let go of your anger
let go of your smallness
causing your very being
to be heavy

with sickness
never again
carry such heavy weight
let your heart be free
from such darkness

sarah slowly sitting up
lighter
bathed in the fragrance
of jesus' healing presence
the darkness
having been absorbed
by the oil
sarah looking intensely at jesus
friend
when you first walked
into this room
was the first time
felt i could let go
of all these poisonous feelings
contained
within my heart
time after time
my daughter told me
to let go
of the bitterness
    the hate
caused by such small petty people
but i couldn't
until i felt you put
    the oil on my forehead
    it unloosened

what was hardened
in my heart
i forgave those
who have damaged me
as i did this
i began to feel
better and better
when you took my hands
rubbed the oil
i could let go
of all the negative feelings
that were destroying me
friend of peter
thank you
for healing me
helping me let go
of all that was causing me
to lie in bed
day after day
may never again
my heart be ruled
by negativity
let me remember
your healing touch
the smell of this oil fragrant

now
jesus handing me the oil
peter you too
are called
to help others
to leave their places

        of darkness
        of sickness
    let the oil strong
        absorb
        hurtful memories
        bitterness
    so their hearts
        can pump once again
        blood through the whole body
    what happened
    in this once darkened room
    now bright with healing
    peter
    you also have the strength
    to bring this healing
    to others
    learn from this afternoon
        peter
        to be also a healer

reflection questions

1. What causes darkness in my heart? What fears control me? What anger do I hold on to? Whom have I not forgiven? What hurt lives deep within me?

2. Can I let Jesus anoint those places? Let the oil absorb those things that cause darkness in me?

3. Can I anoint others? Can I hear their pains and hurts and show them the compassion of Jesus?

to see

luke 18:35–43

It is 7:30 a.m. in Torrance, California. Oscar is sitting handcuffed in front of me, and he acknowledges that he has seen me. I spoke with his parents before coming into the courtroom. Oscar recently had been moved from Juvenile Hall to the County Jail. His lawyer showed me what was written on his transfer. It is hard for me to believe the accusations since Oscar is a very serious and reflective young man. For many months he had actively participated in the meditation class at Central Juvenile Hall.

This morning I have written out two paragraphs to speak on his behalf. I stand before the judge. I begin by mentioning Oscar's unfair transfer to the County Jail simply because of the attitude of some of the staff. The judge says, "If some of the staff are acting like that, why don't you file a grievance?"

There it was. The world of power and privilege, which will never be able to understand this other world to which Oscar belongs. I tell the judge that a complaint had already been filed but the same behavior continued. What I experienced that Friday morning is something I think about every time I drive by that courthouse. If you have never experienced what another sector of society experiences, you will never be able to see what is before you.

You *think* you see, like the Pharisees *thought* they saw, but you are blind, actually blind, to the other's reality.

The judge thinks he understands the reality of those being locked up, but that day in court helped me to understand the vast chasm between worlds. To see, really see, is a gift we so badly need. The judge reminded me of how hard this really is if we don't walk with people at the base or those who, in some way, have been marginalized.

What made that Friday morning even more tragic was that Oscar was sentenced to life without the possibility of parole. And he was innocent of the crime.

When Jesus drew near to Jericho, a blind man was sitting by the road, begging. As he heard the crowd passing by, he inquired what it was, and they told him that Jesus of Nazareth was going by. Then he cried out, "Jesus, Son of David, have mercy on me!" The people in front scolded him, "Be quiet!" but he cried out all the more, "Jesus, Son of David, have mercy on me!"

Jesus stopped and ordered the blind man to be brought to him, and, when he came near, he asked him, "What do you want me to do for you?" And the man said, "Lord, that I may see!" Jesus said, "Receive your sight, your faith has saved you." And at once the blind man was able to see and he followed Jesus, giving praise to God.

> the sun was hot
>> pouring down its rays
>> darkness for years
>> i have sat

in darkness with my cup
outstretched
receiving enough to survive
i now have my routine
nothing new

nothing different
day after day
grateful
for the few friends
who support me
when things get rough
jesus passing by
his name
being called out
sitting in darkness
no light
only darkness
jesus coming closer
you could hear
the crowds nearby
from deep place within yelling
jesus i would like
to see
i go through the day
every day
same routine
wander back
to my empty house
in the night
longing to see
so that life
will have meaning
not just reacting to life
responding
to see
have vision
to know

where i am going
i desired this greatly
i wanted to get
   his attention
jesus
i yelled
as loud as i could
i am over here
jesus
my voice
   sailed through the air
   jesus
   then there was silence
   even the crowd
   was calm silent
   someone sitting down
   next to me
   silence
my name is jesus
how can i help you?
jesus put his hand
   on my shoulder
what is your name?
jesus my name
   is moses
i yelled your name
   to ask you
   if you can help me see
moses
do you really want
to see?
do you really?

to leave
your darkness
what you have
grown accustomed to?
are you ready
to be whole
with sight?
jesus
putting his hands
across my eyes
abba
i see my brother moses here
he has been
in darkness for a long time
to see
to really see
what you want
us to do
abba no matter what
this is difficult
may your healing power
abba
flow into moses
so when he opens
his eyes
and sees
he can really see
not like these pharisees here
who think they can see
for they are much more blind
than moses
to see what you desire

abba
where you want us
to walk
to see you
in great and small moments
of the day
pharisees think they see you
are so convinced
they know the way
they are lost
they can't see
they actually
are stumbling around
all the time
going around in circles
to have eyes to see
is so different
and i ask you also
abba
to give moses
your eyes to see
to see with compassion
to see with love
not just
go through the routine
of the day
not just
merely existing
but with sight
your sight abba
to see
what you desire

to see with the heart
to see what you desire

moses
slowly opening his eyes
at first
only blur
only outline of jesus' face
touching his face
  thank you jesus
  for giving me sight
may i never go back
to live in darkness
joy spread
  through moses' heart
  to see
  really see
while many people
  remain blind
  all their lives

reflection questions

1. In what ways am I blind?

2. Are there people I refuse to see? Who are they? Are there parts of myself I cannot face? What are they?

3. Do I really want to see? To leave what I have grown accustomed to? Am I ready to see what God desires for me?

nets

luke 5:1–11

During his two year stay at Juvenile Hall Ruben was a bright light. He is a born leader. If not in prison, no doubt he would be on the city council. He participated in many of the activities at Juvenile Hall, especially in theater. He could act and speak effortlessly. He also joined the meditation group. Ruben had been involved in a shooting.

I sat with Ruben one Wednesday night. The next day he needed to decide whether he was going to take the deal he was offered.

The district attorney was offering him eighteen years. He told me that he thought he would go to court, fight his case, and win. What did I think? I was telling myself not to be so foolish as to try to talk this young man out of what he was thinking. I had my own opinion, but I also realized the seriousness of this decision. If he lost he would never see the world with free eyes; if he won he would go home. I remember saying, "Ruben, you need to listen to your heart and ask what God desired for you." We meditated, trying to enable him to get to a level where he could hear the soft voice of what he desired and at the same time the voice of God. What decision was going to give him the most life? To make any decision is a very complex matter.

Ideally, the weeks that these youth practice contemplative prayer gives them the capacity to move to a place where they experience some peace. Contemplation can take them to a place in which they are aware of what is working within them, a place in which they are able to listen to subtle movements within their hearts.

Ruben made his decision and the right one. He wisely took the deal. Ruben learned at an early age not to exclude God from a decision that will affect the rest of his life.

One day, as Jesus stood by the Lake of Gennesaret, with a crowd gathered around him listening to the word of God, he caught sight of two boats left at the water's edge by the fishermen now washing their nets. He got into one of the boats, the one belonging to Simon, and asked him to pull out a little from the shore. There he sat and continued to teach the crowd.

When he had finished speaking he said to Simon, "Put out into deep water and lower your nets for a catch." Simon replied, "Master, we worked hard all night and caught nothing. But if you say so, I will lower the nets." This they did and caught such a large number of fish that their nets began to break. They signaled their mates in the other boat to come and help them. They came and helped fill both boats to sinking point.

Upon seeing this, Simon Peter fell at Jesus' knees, saying, "Leave me, Lord, for I am a sinful man!" For he and his companions were exceedingly amazed at the catch they had made; and so were Simon's partners James and

John, Zebedee's sons. Jesus said to Simon, "Do not be afraid. You will catch people from now on." So they brought their boats to land and followed him, leaving everything.

> the length of the lake
> stretched on forever
> parts were deeper
> dark blue
> reflection from the sky
> all last night
> in the very heart
> of darkness
> we threw in our nets
> again and again
> into the night
> nets hitting the lake
> splashing
> sinking down
> hands
> waiting to see
> if nets would be successful
> the moon was strong
> we kept moving slowly
> across the surface of the lake
> hoping we would be lucky
> as we threw nets in
> again my mind wandered
> back to the intensity
> of these past days
> the problems
> the difficulties

even though we were
not catching anything
was so much easier this fishing
than getting entangled
in the challenges of jesus
daily presented to us
birds following our boat
diving in and out
feeling
at the same time
that even though
these nets were finding
no luck
in the lake's water
how lucky
i have been
to have met
someone like jesus
every day
that i walked with him
i was moved amazed
by who he is
it was time to wander back
to the nearby shore
could see from here
in the boat
a crowd had already
been gathering
waiting to hear some more
from this one from nazareth
as the sun slowly rose
spreading intense rays

across the surface
of the lake
we landed
sitting for a while
watching jesus begin
to speak
once again
something strong
broke open within
just watching jesus
as he reached out
to all gathered
at the shore
they were hungry
looking for something
they were finding this
in jesus
watching all this
i began to feel overwhelmed
too many people
crowding around jesus
getting out of the boat
jesus stopping
approaching me
asking if
i would let him
speak from the boat
feeling once again
fortunate
of course jesus
hours of jesus speaking
to the crowds

passing quickly
finally jesus sitting down
peter
i would like
to help you now
let's catch some fish
i laughed
jesus it honors me
to be with you
as you reach out
to all these good people
but jesus
i'm the fisherman
it is too late
in the day
to catch fish
never
jesus looked at me
smiled
let's go

yes jesus
let's try to catch some fish
taking the oar
rowing fast unevenly
sliding across the lake's surface
sliding
sweat pouring down my face
jesus
coming over
to where
i was so frenetically

rowing
putting his hand
over mine
suddenly changing the rhythm
of working
not with so many jerks
wanting
just to get to where?
now with smooth movements
back and forth
putting the oar
into water
again and again
feeling jesus
next to me
now the rowing
did not take
so much effort
we were making
good progress
and i was enjoying it
so much more
than when i was straining
senselessly
also feeling
a closeness
working like this
with jesus
glancing
over at jesus
could sense
how much

he was enjoying the rowing
after speaking all morning
jesus was relaxing
really liked
how jesus worked
did things
he kept challenging me
in my way of rushing
feeling overwhelmed
by everything
sitting in that boat
rowing out
to the middle
of the lake
feeling a deep presence
remembering
when i was eight
i went to the synagogue
to learn the torah
one night
i was walking
under the stars
feeling something open up
deep within me
after studying that day
about the name yahweh
where it came from
i felt that night
under the stars
a deep love
for this yahweh
not just with the head

but a presence
took hold of me
shook me
left me
different
today in this moment
i feel that presence
rowing out
with jesus
i do what i do
because of the love
that shapes my heart
looking
into jesus' eyes
feeling strongly
this same presence expanding
love filling the heart

jesus stopped rowing
halting the movement of the boat
we were almost
in the middle of the lake
looking into the far distance
seeing outline of shore
there was a stillness
about the moment
no longer
the sound of oars
hitting water
rather now
a silence
jesus gazing around the lake

i could not tell
where he wanted us
to throw in the nets
why did we stop
at this spot?
jesus
gazing into the water
near the back
of the boat
jesus quietly saying
throw in the nets
over there
thinking to myself
as i grabbed
the edges of the nets
sometimes
it seems so difficult
during the day
to know
where to stop the boat
what is the right spot
to catch fish
he knew

jesus
i need to remember
this moment
help me
not to forget
to ask you
where?
where are the fish?

you are not even a fisherman
and yet you know
need to ask your help
to know
what is beneath the surface
jesus
all last night
we stopped
in this same boat
to fish
all last night
i tried
just relied
on my own power
jesus
what happens
when i only rely
on my own self?
lifting the nets
all of us in the boat
jesus next to me
then casting nets
onto surface of still lake
falling into the dark blue
deeper and deeper
waiting
suddenly tug on the hand
soon could tell
the nets were filling
with fish swarming
jesus
there are so many places

we could have stopped
but it is only here
there is found
such abundance
of fish
this spot
how to tell
if this is the spot
to find fish
in what i do
in a day
all the activities
the movements
the planning
always wondering
if this is the spot?
if this is the place
where you want me
to be?
i ask myself
again and again
this question
if this is the spot
help me jesus
to learn
this fishing skill
to know
where you want me
to stop the boat
and throw in the nets
to find
fish abundant

wondering
if finding the spot
catching fish
makes any difference
to you master
jesus took his hand
away from the net's edge
moved closer
to where i was
does it make
any difference?
peter i saw
how you helped
the many fishermen yesterday
saw you last night
go out to fish
felt grateful this morning
when you lent me
your boat
does what you do
affect
touch me?
peter
i am moved
by you
by what you do
large warm tears
falling down peter's cheeks
jesus
putting his arm
around peter
as the nets becoming fuller

peter
how can i tell you
how what you do
i appreciate it
in many ways
in fact
peter when we finish
with this catch
i would like
to talk to you
about a different kind of job
feeling pull of fish
feeling a warmth in my heart
the hours that i have walked
with jesus
helped him in hard situations
felt good
to know
that this was important
to the one
who knows
where the fish are
feeling something
so much greater
taking place
in this spot
standing next to jesus
he was helping me
to see below the surface
to see this deeper level
in our lives
that life

does not consist
in going through mechanical motions
but rather
it's all about
why we do
what we do
what is the motivating force
moving us
to do what we do
to the most humble
to the most grandiose
what counts is the love
and how
on this deeper level
our works our actions
can give pleasure
give joy
to the one
who made all this
was now time to pull
in the nets
we all concentrated
bringing in such a catch
working with compañeros
feeling the joy
that comes from this work
done in collaboration
done in unison
experiencing
for one pure moment
the satisfaction
of working together

effortlessly
lifting such a catch
into the boat
knew this feeling
would not last long
good to enjoy the moment
so when other trying ones come
will remember
back to this moment
of joyfully working together

the nets were heavy now
against the hands
never did i think
we would catch fish
with the sun so high
the nets were overflowing
with large fish
jesus saying
peter come closer
put your feet
against this side
of the boat
moved closer
to jesus
felt as if again
nets sinking down
deeper and deeper
this time
it was happening
within
to be closer

to you jesus
to move closer
to bring in this catch
my arms were aching
from the impossible weight
of the catch
we're going to need help
from the other boats
two motions
at the same time
one growing closer to jesus
the other the pressure
against the fingers
the cords burning
palms of hand
the weight of the catch
had reached
the point of being impossible
to bring in
was too overbearing
too much
jesus
this is how
much of the time
life seems
impossible
with so much pressure
pulling against us
so many times
while fishing jesus
don't know
how i will have the strength

to bring in the catch
all the impossible situations
feeling at this moment
jesus
i would like to be closer
to you
not just because
you have great fishing instincts
but because i feel
you are inviting me
to this way of fishing
to enter into closer friendship
with you
standing next to jesus
pulling hard against
the cords
sweat pouring profusely
peter
you're right
remember
when we finish here
we'll talk
don't try to do it alone
any longer peter
the weight of the nets
pulling against the hands
was not any less
with jesus
next to me
pulling
but something was different
working together

using all our strength
jesus am grateful
for this day
i thought i was just going
back to my house to sleep
but am grateful
for what you are teaching me

reaching shore
cleaning nets
that held so many fish
folding them
placing them carefully
in the boat
sitting down on the sand
gazing out at the lake
felt good
having caught such a catch
thinking of jesus' fishing instincts
when his shadow
passed over
where i was sitting
jesus
sitting down next to me
peter
what did you think
of fishing today?
remember
i wanted to ask
you something
when we finished
with the fishing

yes jesus
of course
i remember this
well peter
i would like you
to be a fisherman
in a different way
i would like you
to help me
in building
the reign of yahweh
helping others
grow get closer
to the one greater
jesus
to help
in a project
to make this
a better country?
a work
that would lead others
to know yahweh
more closely?
jesus
i'm just a poor fisherman
don't have skills
to accomplish
that kind of project
peter
i have a question for you
what did it feel like
rowing out to the middle

of the lake
with me?
throwing in the nets?
feeling the pulls
on the hands
from such a large catch?
jesus
i liked very much
working with you
today
from early this morning
i watched the faces
of those gathered
at the shore
they were moved
by what was said
you gave them hope
felt that yahweh
was with us
today
but to help you?
yet jesus
i felt different today
that this really might
be possible
a love took over the heart
connected
to yahweh leading his people
from egypt
to freedom
to help you jesus?
so that others can

really feel this love
that their lives
will be different
how they see things
what they do
will be different
because of this love
of yahweh
jesus what can i say
to you?
yes jesus
i'll follow you
help you
with this project

reflection questions

1. Do I sometimes work frenetically and all alone? in my work? in my home? in my relationships? Have I ever tried to change my rhythm? Can I let Jesus change my rhythm?

2. Do I forget to ask Jesus, "Where are the fish? Where do you want me to be?"

3. How do I remain open to seeing "below the surface, to see this deeper level in our lives"? Do I remember to ask Jesus to show me that deeper place?

4. Am I being called to work with Jesus? In what way do I experience that call? Can I sense that I am good enough to do God's work?

stars

matthew 14:22–23

Richard is seventeen years old. He has been incarcerated for seven long months. He was baptized during one of the weekly liturgies we have in the gym on Sundays. On a Wednesday, I came early so he could have some time for the Sacrament of Reconciliation.

The following week I invited thirty young men present in the unit to celebrate Reconciliation. Richard stood up in the group and said, "I feel different after confessing. I now no longer feel the pressure about what I have done. I have never talked to anyone seriously about what has happened in my life. I feel all around better. I know that since God has forgiven me, He will put in the heart of anyone else whom I have hurt to also forgive me. It was just good to talk to someone you can say everything to." He let out a deep breath and added, "You will all feel better if you do."

That evening many of the youth decided to frequent this sacrament because of the testimony of Richard. Driving home that night I was thinking of the unbelievable power of this sacrament. I was glad that Richard could somehow feel what it is to be forgiven and that others were encouraged to do the same.

Immediately Jesus made his disciples get into the boat and go ahead of him to the other side, while he sent the crowd away. And having sent the people off, he went up the mountain by himself to pray. At nightfall, he was there alone.

        needed to be alone
        to be alone
        after being with people
          all day
        all afternoon was looking forward
        to go up the mountain
        to be with my abba
        my body breathed out
        the stillness
        of the night
        looking up at the galaxies
        stars covering the whole night sky
        breathing in the mystery
          grandeur
        of being in the solitude
        of this spot
        slowly
        from a very deep place
        praying
          abba
          feeling you abba
          close
          as i look up
          at the brilliance
          of these millions of stars
          dancing around and around

abba
just need to be
in this solitary spot
away from the crowds
away from everyone
just sitting here
calling your name
abba
in the darkness
of the night
my spirit feels overwhelmed
as far as the eye
can wander
bright shining stars
abba
this mystery fills me with awe
i reach up
and touch your face
and you wrap your presence
around me
my heart is full
in this solitude
feel as if abba
i could stay here
forever
breathing in your presence
mystery
flowing through me
in this darkness
of the middle of the night
is connected
to everything abba

that has happened
during this week
my heart beats faster
as the faces
of so many appear
feeling in this
an even greater mystery
than the star-studded sky
    abba
    i utter your name
    and it is lost
    in the stars
    and yet you are here
    by my side
    abba
    i sit here
    looking into lighted space
    i walked yesterday
    to capernaum
    peter had asked me
    to speak with
    the son of his neighbor
    i walked over
    where the romans held him
    he is fifteen
    rufus

when i walked into his cell
rufus could not look at me
feeling same thing
as i feel
in this moment

great mystery
feeling your presence
i asked how he was
and he began to look at me
for a long time
we did not say anything
not one word
at the right moment
  i asked him
  what happened?
  what happened?
slowly he talked about
how it was late at night
he was angry
at his classmate simon
who stole his money
that he had worked for all year
in the cover of darkness
he waited for him
to return to his house
rufus jumped him
he was just planning
to get back his money
but rufus
took out his knife
in a moment of anger-hate
he stabbed simon
he remembered seeing his face
as he fell
to the ground
blood flowing out of his mouth
rufus didn't want to kill him

that had not been his intention
he just wanted revenge
the other fell to the ground
his face contorted
anguish
pain
shooting out
rufus's hand was covered
with blood
the one lay dying
hardly breathing now
rufus
felt a sick feeling
tear at him
from within
he wanted to vomit
rufus watched as life
poured out of simon
at this moment
from behind
a band of roman soldiers
captured him

as rufus finished
telling this event
he put his head
into his hands
and wept loudly
long hot tears
flowed down his cheeks
   i wake up
   every night in a cold sweat

    i see the expression
    on simon's face
    after i stabbed him
    i can't breathe
    in that moment
    never wanted to kill him
    was that really me
    who stuck the knife
    into his heart?
    don't know what to do
jesus breathing in even more deeply
the mystery of being
in the mystery of his abba
peering up
as stars fell
out of the heavens
shooting rapidly
across the sky
to be here
on this mountain
in the solitude
in the presence
of his abba
knowing
soon he would need
to give his disciples a hand
on the lake
but now
he needed to pray
    abba one greater
    i felt powerless
    yesterday

in that moment with rufus
i put my arms
around his shoulders
and let him
cry some more
really didn't need
to say anything
there was a stillness
a depth
abba
just like now with you
yesterday the feelings
that permeated
the prison cell
the realization
of the utter seriousness
of ending the life
of another
and the loss
that simon's parents
brothers and sisters experienced
after his body had no more life
the future for simon
now ended
was no more
no more school
no more friends
no more anything
memory of blood flowing
from simon's mouth
taking away someone's dreams
ending possibilities

of ever being a husband father
in five short minutes
everything was different
forever changed
irrevocably
a heaviness filled the cell
jesus
remembering
how he put his hands
on top of rufus's head
giving him the strength
to pray
   with many tears
   and a wounded heart

   yahweh
   as a small child
   i was taught
   to respect life
   to be good
   i come to you
   at this moment
   to ask you yahweh
   to forgive me
   for taking the life
   of simon
   i don't know
   why i did it
   i wish
   with all my heart
   i could take back
   those five minutes

but i know
that can't happen
i ask you yahweh
i ask his family
to forgive me

at this precise moment
it was as if
a long stream of cold water
shot through rufus's body
starting
from jesus' fingers
down his head
into his heart
through his feet
into the ground
as if a cleansing deep
permitting the caked dirt
to be washed
onto the ground
jesus
feeling this cleansing
praying
gently
   abba
   i pray for
   my brother rufus here
   what he has done
   is unfathomable
   mysteriously incomprehensible
   i feel abba
   that rufus's sorrow is genuine

his contrition is true
as his tears
show
not coming from a superficial place
of getting caught
but of making
a horrible mistake
causing
untold painful consequences
for others
who knew
and loved simon
abba
loving forgiving one
i ask you
to forgive rufus
receiving this prayer
strong red currents
exploding
in rufus's heart
forgiven
forgiven
exploding
feeling an overbearing weight
being released
as forgiveness
resounded within
to begin anew
to be forgiven
no more nightmares
no more cold sweats
after this feeling

of release
of forgiveness
the power
of being forgiven
jesus
looking up
at the stars huddled together
in galaxies
vast beyond comprehension
mystery of this universe
encompassing
to be forgiven
by one who gave life
who is life
and to be repentant
so deeply
that the one who gives life
can release
from one
who took away life
can give this one
another life
by beginning again

rufus opening his eyes
feeling
as if waking up
from a dream
this time
not from a nightmare
but from a dream
that changed his life forever

>   jesus
>   thank you
>   for forgiving me
>   for forgiving me
>   jesus
>   remembering all this
>   from the day before
>   in the solitude
>   of this mountain
>   jesus
>   feeling his abba very close
>   feeling so strongly
>   the power of forgiveness

reflection questions

1. Have I felt as powerless as Jesus did in the moment with Rufus? What was that moment like? Was God there? How did I experience the presence or the absence of God?

2. Are there "five minutes" in my life in which I did something that I wish I could take back? What was it that I did? Have I asked for forgiveness?

3. Do I really believe that Abba can forgive all? How do I experience forgiveness in my life? Where do I need forgiveness in my life?

impossible

matthew 14:24–33

I arrive at the High Risk Unit of Juvenile Hall on Sunday at 8:30 a.m. I sit with Marlon, who is going to court the next day to be sentenced. He is distracted, not able to focus on our conversation. Marlon looks stressed. He has taken a deal for nine years, and tomorrow he will be sentenced for his crime of armed robbery. He does not want to talk about it.

During the years I've worked at the detention center, I have seen young men change, but I have never seen anything like the transformation that took place within Marlon. During the past months we had spent many long hours talking about how he ended up in a gang, about his family and his dreams. His face showed the sincerity of his desire to make something of his life, if only he would be given another chance. I asked Marlon if he wanted me to go to court with him the next day. He said that it wouldn't do any good, but if I wanted to, okay.

The next day I arrived at court, and finally after two hours of waiting, it was Marlon's turn. He was very serious and spoke to the attentive judge from the heart. Then it was my turn to speak. I looked at the judge and said, "Your Honor, I believe this young man deserves another chance. As Marlon himself says, the man you see

today is a man much changed from the one who com-
mitted the crime." The judge sentenced him to five years
in the Youth Authority. The lessening of a sentence, once
you have taken a deal, almost never happens. It seemed
impossible, but it happened.

The following week Marlon wrote a piece in his writing class about a miracle: "The D.A. wanted me to get more time. His attempt failed. The judge overruled his argument. The judge said, 'I'm giving you a walk in the park Mr. R., considering you could have lost over thirty years of your life for this crime. But I have a feeling that you will make something of your life.' I knew that a miracle had occurred."

Marlon went to Youth Authority and received straight A's while attending university classes. He received a full scholarship to Santa Clara University.

Meanwhile, the boat was by now very far from the land, dangerously rocked by the waves for the wind was against it. By daybreak, Jesus came to them walking on the lake. When they saw him walking on the lake, they were terrified, thinking that it was a ghost. And they began to cry. But at once Jesus said to them, "Courage! Do not be afraid, it is I." Peter answered, "Lord, if it is you, command me to come to you walking on the water."

Jesus said to him, "Come." And Peter got out of the boat, walking on the water to go to Jesus. But, in face of the strong wind, he was afraid and began to sink. So he cried out, "Lord, save me!" Jesus immediately stretched out his hand and took hold of him, saying, "Man of little faith, why did you doubt?" When they got into the boat, the wind ceased. Then those in the boat bowed before Jesus saying, "Truly, you are the Son of God!"

looking up
at the stars
feeling strong wind
reflecting
on the powerful feelings
i had with jesus and the crowd
yesterday
i was so afraid
of what was going
to happen
afraid
because we had no money
no food
and a huge crowd hungry
not having eaten
all day
why have i been so afraid
during these last months?
as i was rocked
back and forth
with the motion
of the boat
reflecting
on so many things
have been afraid of
now once again
a fear began to grow within
as the wind
grew stronger and stronger
why did jesus

leave us alone?
thinking hard about storms
on this lake
when a bright light suddenly
appeared to my right
my hands gripped
hard
the sides of the boat
how many dead fishermen
haunted the depths
of this lake?
who was now returning
to haunt us?
ghost-like figure coming
closer and closer
fear paralyzing me
coming closer and closer
was this going to be the night
when these waters
would also receive me
into the depths?
as suddenly
as this ghost-like figure
appeared in the distance
the bright blur gave shape
to a familiar face
there he was in front of me
but my fright
still ruled my heart
jesus
approaching the boat
wind strong

courage peter
it is i
do not be afraid

don't be afraid?
jesus
i first feel
as if we are
going to drown
then i think
i see a ghost
and you tell me
not to be afraid
jesus i would like to leave
all this fear
in the boat
i would like to come to you
if it is really you
let me come closer to you

peter
come here
felt moved by this invitation
looking
at the waves high
seeing the peaceful face of jesus
so different from the violence
of the wind
there was a warmth
found in his eyes
could see clearly
jesus standing on the water
he was holding out

his hands
come peter
i started to lift myself up
do i trust you enough
to face this raging wind
darkened forces?
do i?
my heart won
i found myself
locked in jesus' gaze
warm inviting look
i was lost
in this moment
my feet guiding me
along the surface
of white-crested water
gazing at jesus
why had i let fear
take over
during the night?
looking
directly into the eyes of jesus
feeling confident
feeling connection strong
i could do it
i could do it
feeling this
looked into one of the waves
felt the rush of the wind
against my tunic
now staring directly
into dark water

no longer
with my eyes focused on jesus
once again
ghost-like fear
gripped hard my heart
who am i
to be able to walk
on water?
all my self doubts
my weaknesses
pulled me as forcefully
into the water
as the strength of howling wind
trying hard in resisting
as the forces
of the underworld
tried to bring me
into its grip
why did i ever
take my eyes
off you jesus?
why?
why does fear
always seem to be winning?
i thought jesus
i could really this time
trust you
i felt this as long
as i kept my eyes
looking into your face
now all i see
is darkness

was being swallowed
up by fear
knew
i had one last moment
before i would forever
be lost
in this vortex
of darkness
beginning to swallow
the water
pulling me down
deeper and deeper
jesus i cried
i'm going to die
i'm going to drown
can't see anything
please help me
help me jesus
my cry
was carried
by the gusts of wind
couldn't see anything
but i felt
a strong grip
grab my hand
as he rescued me
from these raging waters
feeling a sense of relief
feeling secure
in the embrace of jesus
jesus thank you
for helping me

to be saved
from the water
my body still shaking
from this near-death-moment
beginning to breathe again
in the embrace of jesus
letting out
all the water
i had swallowed
as i struggled
to come back
jesus i took
my eyes from you
i feel exhausted
but being close
to you again
tell you jesus
i do want to learn
how to walk on water
i start
to think of the impossible parts
of my life
as if there will never
be a solution to the problem
as if things will only get worse
or like yesterday
impossible
to feed all the people
it was impossible
truly impossible
but jesus with you
it was not impossible

with you
we walked on water
as we gave food
to all those present
impossible to accomplish
what we needed to do
was impossible
with you jesus
it was possible
jesus
i want so much
to walk on water
again and again
don't want the thoughts
of how impossible tasks are
to distract me again
jesus
that is why
i have enjoyed walking
with you
you try to teach me
how to walk on water
every day
but i always
let the thoughts
of how it is not possible
destroy the lesson
jesus
bringing me gently
back to the boat
sitting down
exhausted

discouraged
yet feeling
i am not really ready
to give up
learning
to walk on water
one day i will not let
negative thoughts
doubts
fear
ghosts
take over
and i really will
keep me eyes on you
and learn to walk on water
to where you will be standing
waiting with open arms

reflection questions

1. In what ways am I invited by Jesus to "walk on water"? Do I believe I can do it? Do I doubt myself? How do my doubts keep me from "walking on water"?

2. "Do I trust you enough to face this raging wind, these darkened forces?"

3. Do I let "thoughts of how impossible tasks are" distract me? When have I done that recently? Can I again imagine that same situation, but now going through it keeping my eyes on Jesus?

time

luke 11:38-42

Elizabeth, one of the girls in Juvenile Hall, was baptized this year. Her sponsor, Laura, gave her a copy of some meditations I had written. After she read some of them, Elizabeth told Laura that she would like to talk to me. She wanted to speak about her experiences of God.

When I met her, she talked about how God is working in her life. Sometimes Elizabeth can't sleep thinking about all the time she is going to be locked up. She gets too stressed out to fall asleep. When she meditates, she feels that Jesus is right there. She likes to talk about what happens in her prayer. Elizabeth is very serious about developing her inner life.

How many times during these last couple of years have I sat with sixteen- or seventeen-year-olds, realizing the amount of time they will spend behind bars? The potential to grow spiritually is great and the potential to enter into darkness is also great. Until recently, I had never thought about how the word "mystical" can be attached to those in prison. After listening to Elizabeth and others like her, I realize that the invitation to deep inner life is possible and very powerful for them. Their external world has been very much reduced, almost like those in monasteries, and with this comes the potential to develop other dimensions of the person, to go inward and from this to be able to live in prison with tranquility.

This type of religious conversation with persons like Elizabeth is not like our usual lunch conversations. An atmosphere of trust is created in those moments in which religious conversation happens very naturally. I hope that for the next twelve years Elizabeth's deep inner life can grow in her new monastery.

As Jesus and his disciples were on their way, he entered a village and a woman called Martha welcomed him to her house. She had a sister named Mary, who sat down at the Lord's feet to listen to his words. Martha, meanwhile, was busy with all the serving, and finally she said, "Lord, don't you care that my sister has left me to do all the serving?"

But the Lord answered, "Martha, Martha, you worry and are troubled about many things, whereas only one thing is needed. Mary has chosen the better part, and it will not be taken away from her."

> i had to finish cleaning
> the other room
> as i did this
> my thoughts turned to how
> i needed to bring out the clothes
>   all this whirled around
>   as i ran up and down
>   the stairs

sweat pouring down my forehead
wanted to stop
and sit with my two neighbors
who rested
under the trees below
but i could not spare
the time
in no way
for soon i would need
to be in the kitchen
preparing food
always seems
my life is weighted down
by so many responsibilities
watched
as my neighbors
drank
their cool drinks
why was i so disturbed
as they enjoyed the moment?
i was too busy
to enjoy anything
  inside myself
  on some level
  wishing for a change
  knowing
  life can be different
  different
  hearing loud knocking
    downstairs
  inside felt
  how i did not want

to be disturbed
because i had
too much work
more than
i could accomplish
in three mornings
waiting to see
  if my sister
  would answer the door
  but not the case
  hurriedly
  i rushed down the stairs
    to see
    who was so intensely
    knocking
    at the front door
  how do my neighbors
  live without pressure?

arriving at the wooden door
slowly opening the door
directly in front
was a small group
my brother
  was with them
  looked
  into the face of jesus
  his eyes
  were tired
  could tell
  this group had walked
  all morning

there was a weariness
that hung over them
quickly opening my mouth
   jesus
   good to see you
   welcome to our house
   i was just cleaning
   now i will begin cooking
   there will be sufficient
   for all of you
am glad you will be
a guest
in our home
you are most welcome
   martha
   good to see you
   hope we are not disturbing you
   we were passing through here
   on our way to jerusalem
   at this moment
   my sister mary joined us
   welcoming jesus
   with a wide embrace
   let's go inside
   to the coolest room
   jesus
   passing through the door
   as i looked
   into his weary face
   knew i could change
   entering the dark cool room
   water flowing over rocks

all sitting down
listening to this one
entering the room
sitting there for a few moments
knowing i needed
to go to the kitchen
to prepare
for so many people
even though
i knew
this was really the place
to be
there was no doubt
in my mind
that i needed
to hear this master speak
watched my sister mary
remain behind
at the threshold
i caught the words
jesus was speaking
felt as if he were speaking to me
felt pulled to go to the kitchen
felt pulled to the room
i couldn't decide
so i remained in the doorway
staring at jesus
as he spoke
i wanted to stay and listen
but felt pulled
into the kitchen
felt obligated

even though
my heart was telling
me something different
that i should stay
how do i change?
how can i ever just
stay and enjoy presence?
felt driven
by so many inner voices
felt i was not enjoying
anything i was doing
this even made me feel worse
   watched jesus
   from the doorway
   laughing
   speaking of
   this morning's journey
   with his friends
wanted so much to join them
but i didn't
i hurried to the kitchen
soon i was immersed
in my world of preparing food
how many were there?
was there enough food?
did not know
asking myself the whole time
why i was not able
to stay and listen
speak to jesus?
i was enjoying
the encounter

the time of preparing the food
was over
felt upset restless
resented so much
my sister was not here
helping me
felt angry at everyone
    at everyone
time to announce
the food was ready
i walked into the room
with a heavy heart
jesus looked up
at me
the way he read me
signaled me to sit
next to him
as the water flowed
next to us
he asked me
a simple question
what's wrong?
i looked around me
everyone relaxed
their faces glowed
from the enjoyment
of spending this time
together

why couldn't i enter
into this dance of the moment?
what was stopping me?

jesus
before the sun rose
i was up cleaning this house
i had ordered the supplies
by seven
prepared breakfast
by eight
worked on the books
until ten
washed clothes
until you came
jesus just looking at me
suddenly
he smiled
a smile as wide
as our desert terrain
in that moment
i felt ridiculous
about what i was saying
i laughed out loud
jesus knew also
this cool room
lit up
with pure enjoyment
  i understood
  i finally understood
what i was feeling
  as i stood at the doorway
  knew i was being changed
  never again
  would i leave
  the moment

when my heart
tells me to be here
   never again
would i refuse
to enjoy the moment
with my neighbors
with my piled-up-high excuses
of how much i need to do
   never again
would i be resentful
   at others who know
how to enjoy life
   to begin again
   to do a few things
   to enjoy each one
   that is what
   i was feeling
   enjoying the moment
   nothing to do
   even though
   there was everything to do
   pressures
   demands
   whirled off me
   as i was present
   in this circle of enjoyment
   tomorrow
   i would sit
with my neighbors
as they enjoy
the morning shade
i would learn to walk

to places
i have never been
because i have been too busy
i will do few things
and enjoy each one
this master from nazareth
was showing me
so simply
how to really do this
enjoy the moment

reflection questions

1. Do I have an endless list of things to do? Am I focused on the list? Do I focus on the moment when all of the things will be done instead of living in the present moment?

2. How might I practice living in the present? What are some of the things that take me out of the present?

3. Do I enjoy life? How do I express my enjoyment? How might I begin to enjoy life?

anointing

mark 14:3–9

It is now eight o'clock on a Tuesday night in January. I am at a retreat house in Encino helping to give a retreat for chaplains from all over the Los Angeles Archdiocese who work in detention ministry. During these last two days, I have time and again been moved by the stories from these good people doing such important work. I feel privileged to be here.

It is time for the liturgy. The theme is healing. I begin the liturgy by telling how at the prayer service on Wednesdays at our parish, sometimes people say, "Padre, as a minister, you also need to be anointed and healed." So each week I put out my hands, find myself also vulnerable, needing the healing touch of God as much as anyone else.

I ask the chaplains this night to allow themselves to be ministered to, especially after ministering to so many in painful situations. I begin putting warm scented oil, in the sign of a cross, on their hands. I rub the oil on the hands of George, who works in the County Jail. The story he shared in the afternoon came alive in that moment. Two rival gang members were put together in the hospital unit of the county jail. One of the gang members, whose gang was responsible for the death of one in the other gang, was rolled in, totally at the mercy of those around him

since he was paralyzed and could not feed himself. What was going to happen? The rival gang member went and started to feed him.

I finish the anointing. We join hands to pray. A deep silence penetrates. It is good to receive this anointing, to be ministered to by each other after having daily ministered to countless persons whose lives have been so broken.

Jesus was in Bethany in the house of Simon the leper. He was at dinner when a woman entered carrying a precious jar of expensive perfume made of pure nard. She broke the jar and poured the perfumed oil on Jesus' head. Then some of them became angry and said, "What a useless waste of perfume. It could have been sold for more than three hundred silver coins and the money given to the poor." And they criticized her.

But Jesus said, "Let her alone; why are you troubling her? What she has just done for me is a very charitable work. At any time you can help the poor, for you always have them with you, but you will not have me forever. This woman has done what was hers to do; she has anointed my body in anticipation of my burial. Truly, I say to you, wherever the Good News is proclaimed all over the world, what she has done will be told in praise of her."

> i was walking
>   through the center
>   of the plaza
>   confident in myself

good business last night
four high-paying customers
just finished
  buying freshly baked bread
  when i dropped a package
  as i came up
  from picking it up
  caught sight of one passing
  his gaze caught me
  did not think much
  of this glance
but asking one
  next to me
  who is this one?
  he certainly
  is not from the city
  but somewhere
  in the country
that's jesus
he's from nazareth
many say he can cure
  heal
all kinds of sicknesses
  these words
  stayed within me
  jesus of nazareth
maybe he can heal the heart
ever since
  i can remember
  my heart has been torn apart
  walking back
  to my house

watching neighbors stare at me
because of what i was wearing
always feel so judged
from this self-righteous group
they were excitedly
  talking about
  how this very evening
simon
had invited the healer
  to his home
  i had four appointments
  later in the evening
  ate a light meal
  the face of jesus stayed with me
  around and around
i ventured forth
  from my home
  in order to catch
  another glimpse of him
  brought my best oil
  to anoint his feet
closing the door
  to my house
have i really ever
  heard anyone
  say they love me?
only falsely uttered
in the highest passion
closing tight the door
as i neared
simon's stately house
wondered

what was i doing
going where decent people
dine?
who am i to dare enter
this kind of house?
  once again
  my hand on a door latch
  this time
  to open a door
  even though
  on almost every level
  wanted to turn back
  not open this door
  any wider
  something greater
  pulled me
  gave me strength
  to open
  this large wooden door
  opening wide
letting in the smells
  the soft light
  the rich music
as i entered the dining room
  every head turned
  in disbelief except one
i made my way
  over to where jesus sat
  i no longer cared
  what others thought
i knelt down
in front of jesus

tears of great emotion
filling my eyes
jesus
  i was scared
  to come here
  when i stood up
    yesterday
  and gazed
  into your face
something happened
  within me
my whole body shaking
  uncontrollably now
jesus stood by me
  placing his strong hands
  on my shoulders
jesus
  i don't know what to say
  have been used
  and supposedly loved by men
  for so many years
  night after night
  but kneeling in front of you
i honestly tell you jesus
  i feel something
  never have felt
  in my whole life
  taking jesus' hands
  into mine
jesus
  i tell you
  this night

as i look into your eyes
as i gaze
into your face
i tell you something
i wanted
to tell someone
all my life
jesus i love you
i know
this as the truest moment
in my life
i love you
feel as if i have known you
all my life
every day
i have really wanted
to say
with the heart
these words
i love you
looked at jesus' eyes
filling with tears
putting his hands
on top
of my head
maria
when i saw you
in the plaza this afternoon
thought
what a good person
she is
but how she has been misled

maria
your abba
loves you without limits
when i say this to you
realize
your abba is saying it
to you
hands warm
on top of my head
maria
i love you
hearing these words from jesus
i love you
first time
in my whole life
someone really said
these words to me
i love you
and meant them
remembering
when i was small
how i longed
for my mother
for my father
to say these simple three words
i feel so different jesus
that someone
has told me this
truly
i love you
not like the cheap way
others have said it

with this love
burning in my heart
i took from my pocket
my precious oil
   i poured some of it
   into my hand
   then gently
   bent down
   took the oil
   rubbed it
   all over jesus' feet
   fragrance strong
   jesus
   i tell you
   have appreciated
   what you have done
   in my heart
   never want to forget
   to thank you
   for your love abundant

maria
remember
this moment
when the one
who made the stars
greater than we can ever imagine
greater
is saying to you
ever so clearly
i love you

reflection questions

1. Am I seeking Jesus? Is there something I desire from Jesus?

2. Do I believe that "the one who made the stars, greater than we can ever imagine, is saying to [me] ever so clearly, I love you." Can I imagine Jesus saying these words to me? What does that feel like?

3. Would it be possible to live always with the awareness that my Abba loves me?

last meal

john 13:1–4

On the second Sunday of every month, the parents of detained youth in Central Juvenile Hall participate in the twelve o'clock liturgy at our parish church, Dolores Mission. Afterward we gather to share a meal. Around the table, the parents talk about what is going on with their sons. The conversations that grow out of the sharing signal the depth of parental concern and love. The parents help each other out just by speaking from the heart.

It is the second Sunday of April. Darío's father brings a picture of his son when he was arrested at fifteen. He was given twenty-nine years to life. Someone asks him how he is doing, and he starts to cry. Feeling this sorrow I think of how the lives of all the family members are changed by having someone incarcerated.

William's mother sits next to Darío's father. She says that many of her friends left her when they found out she has a son who is incarcerated. This is her first time with the group. Her son is finally to be sentenced the following week. This is the first time anything like this has happened to her. She does not know what to do. She is relieved to find a safe place to talk about her feelings with others who have had similar experiences. Her transformed face shows she does not need to give up hope. Her walk is different when she leaves the table after sharing such an enriching meal.

It was before the feast of the Passover. Jesus realized that his hour had come to pass from this world to the Father, and, as he had loved those who were his own in the world, he would love them with perfect love.

They were at supper; the devil had already put into the mind of Judas, son of Simon Iscariot, to betray him, but Jesus knew that the Father had entrusted all things to him and, as he had come from God, he was going to God. So he got up from table, removed his garment, and taking a towel wrapped it around his waist.

> everything was set up
> the candles the serving bowls
> had walked to this room
> alone
> both for safety
> and for time to think
> too much danger lately
> too much pressure
> in trying to keep jesus
> from being arrested
> the tension between
> these city walls was great
> as i walked up the incline
> to this house
> reflected back
> to the first time

i met jesus
i remember that day
so well
the beginning of a friendship
we spent the afternoon
at jesus' house
reflecting as i walked here
for this meal
what this friendship
has meant during these years
just know
that so many times
during these years
sitting around the fire
before we all closed our eyes
we would talk about
what happened
during the day
reflecting somehow
during those moments
he has let me see things
that i would never have seen
he helped me
to understand the meaning
to find the face
of his abba
in the movements
of the day
in the times i felt frustrated
overwhelmed by life's problems
jesus
helped me

to climb out
of the circular mess
have known for many years
so many rabbis
so many religious leaders
many of them so learned
but jesus
is different
feel close to him
has taught me
about the heart
how to forgive my enemies
never thought
i would be able to do this
to forgive the high priests
who threw my family
off their land
because they couldn't pay
unjust taxes they demanded
i had kept hate
inside for so long
before i met jesus
i had so many people
in my life
who i considered enemies
after the romans
killed my brother
   never thought
   i could go to sleep
   without first thinking
   how i could kill
   one of them

i had hate
that ruled without limit
my heart

jesus
saying one time
clearly
to the crowd
that to hate our enemies
is what the pagans do
who wins in this case?
i never
thought i could forgive
my enemies
never ever wanted
to do this
i had grown accustomed
to the hate
i had for my enemies
thought this was normal
that this
is what everyone did
but one day
after jesus spoke
to the crowd
we were sitting
by the river flowing
he talked
about some of the people
who couldn't forgive
their enemies
i was honest

i told jesus
i still had many enemies
and still kept
hate within
he asked me
if i wanted
to let go
of this strong feeling
of killer-like passion
for my enemies
i stopped speaking
wasn't sure
did i really want
to forgive them?
did i?
i told jesus
i wanted to release
the hate in my heart
it was so difficult
having so many enemies
from that day onward
i felt different
  changed
i wanted to forgive
my enemies
and just saying this
began the process
not that it was easy
some days
when i passed a roman
  or high priest
began to get

that old feeling of hate
but by an act of the will
i refused
to let the hate reign
it wasn't
as if i didn't still
have strong negative feelings
those didn't disappear
by forgiving them
rather
i began to see
what jesus
was showing me
that somehow
all of us are connected
if we hate
another person
we are hating ourselves
destroying ourselves
not just the other person
jesus
opened my eyes
to see that everyone
is our brother and sister
at first
i refused to even consider
this idea
but watching jesus
saw how he could deal
with every kind of person
realized
how my friendship

with jesus
was changing me
not just thinking differently
but acting differently
sitting in jesus' house
three years ago
never would have imagined
how changed
a person i would be
because of this friendship
never in my life
   had i understood the power
   of friendship
   the richness
   the depth the joy
   of a friend
   like jesus

the meal beginning
jesus speaking
of how one in our midst
will turn from friend
to one who will betray us
to the authorities
looked at the faces
of my friends
around the table
concern disbelief
i trusted these compañeros
have gone through hardships together
celebrated joyfully with them
and now jesus

was saying one of these
will turn against us
what kind of friend is this?
sharing a meal
then turning his back on us
felt anger within
betray us?
one of our group?
how could this happen?
with others perhaps
but we are the inner circle
the ones of confidence
but this feeling of intimacy
turned to betrayal
turned my stomach
peter
signaling me
to ask jesus
who it is
i moved closer
to jesus
to where we were touching
so i could ask him
  two movements
  passing through my body
  at the same time
  felt jesus close to me
  feeling current of friendship
  of one who understood me
  what i like dislike
  how i feel
  what are my dreams

      the other movement of betrayal
      the opposite of this closeness
jesus
who is going to betray us?
i thought jesus
we were all friends
and only death
could separate us
to be close
to another human
then feel
yourself stabbed
in the back
pain to the heart
confusion
palpitating through veins

jesus whispering
it is the person
   who is handed the bread
judas pulled himself up
   taking the bread
   looked into his eyes
   at that moment
   i felt
   long dormant hate
   swirl up within
   judas
   his eyes already dead
   there was no life in them
   i wanted to jump up
   and seize him

bring him to the floor
but into the darkness
he fled
friend turned betrayer

bringing myself closer to jesus
hot tears
from deepest place
within
needed to feel jesus
close
how is it possible
that judas
could do this?
i considered him
a brother
remember the times
staying awake late at night
he would talk
about his family
about his dreams
he was excited
about the healings
the changes
in the people
we met
but now
felt the door
slammed against my face
the impact
to the heart
was devastating

how can i trust friends
if they can do this to us?

jesus
   is it really judas?
the friends
in our lives
those who are faithful
in good and bad
your friendship
   has changed me
this community of disciples
   of friends
   has changed me
   forever
all i can say
   weakly
is i forgive judas
   if he really is
   the one
   who is going to betray us

reflection questions

1. Is there a hatred within me I would like to let go of? Is there an anger that seethes within that I need to release?

2. Could I bring that hatred or anger before Jesus? Could I let him heal it?

3. Can I forgive and learn to trust again?

washing of feet

john 13:5-15

It is 7:00 p.m., Holy Thursday. This year we selected men from Proyecto Guadalupano to have their feet washed. Proyecto Guadalupano is a program of our parish in which fifty immigrant men are given refuge in the church for three months while they work. These men had walked all day long looking for work, had waited on street corners, and some had actually found work unloading huge crates in the garment district.

Nelson, from El Salvador, is interested in making his first communion while he is staying at the church. He asked me if I wanted to be his *padrino* (godfather) and as a result we had spent time talking together.

Nelson is now sitting in front of the altar with eleven other immigrants. He takes off his shoes and puts his feet on the floor. I take them in my hands and, while pouring the warm water, I remember his story with all the grueling hardships during the two months it took him to get to this country from San Salvador. But what I most remember is the story about how, when he was young, he broke his leg, and his mother couldn't afford crutches for him. She used to carry him, day and night, wherever he needed to go. She did this for six long months.

This image came alive during the footwashing. Now the reason his feet are so dirty is because he has come here to Los Angeles to earn money to send back to El Salvador so his mother can have the operation she needs.

I take the towel and dry his now clean feet. I look up into his face, and he gives me the brightest, warmest smile possible on earth. I feel at that moment how right Jesus is: there is so much joy to be found in being a footwasher.

Then he poured water into a basin and began to wash the disciples' feet and to wipe them with the towel he was wearing.

When he came to Simon Peter, Simon said to him, "Why, Lord, you want to wash my feet!" Jesus said, "What I am doing you cannot understand now, but afterward you will understand it." Peter replied, "You shall never wash my feet." Jesus answered him, "If I do not wash you, you can have no part with me." Then Simon Peter said, "Lord, wash not only my feet, but also my hands and my head!"

Jesus replied, "Whoever has taken a bath does not need to wash (except the feet), for he is clean all over. You are clean, though not all of you." Jesus knew who was to betray him; because of this he said, "Not all of you are clean."

When Jesus had finished washing their feet, he put on his garment again, went back to the table and said to them, "Do you understand what I have done to you? You call me Master and Lord, and you are right, for so I am. If I, then, your Lord and Master, have washed your feet, you also must wash one another's feet. I have just given you an example that as I have done, you also may do."

waiting to see
who climbed the steps
to the upper room
it seemed
no one was watching us
everything ready
inside
nervous energy
around the table
taking off my outer garment
drooping towel over shoulder
going to a small table
at the corner
of the room
picking up large basin
no one seemed
to be paying
much attention to anything
came back
to the larger table
   knelt
   in front of peter
   put your feet
   inside this basin
   i want to clean
   your feet
now every eye
on the room
was focused on us
how hard

it has been
for all my friends
to realize
we are all equal
the power games
played were relentless
the efforts
to be more important
never stopped
so i wanted to give
my friends
an example
with my own life
to wash
dirty feet
to wash feet
putting the towel
over my arm
this thought
of being a footwasher
gave me joy
so many times
after we healed
on the hillside
the crowds wanted
to make me someone
important
in those moments
i always
had this strong love
for my abba
knowing

everything
everything i have
i have received from him
realizing
i was totally dependent
on this love
from my abba
was good
to see faces
relieved from
   so much suffering
healed
of living years in misery
but when they wanted
to seize me
make me their leader
i felt this love
   strong
for my abba
knew
not to be fooled
by these requests
to be famous
how hard
i have tried
during these years
to show
how important it is
not to seek
our own self-importance
for we are
but humble servants

of our abba
who gives all
putting peter's feet in the basin

jesus
what are you doing?
has the pressure
of these days
gotten to you?
what's wrong?
you're our master
only servants wash
other people's feet
i can't let
you wash my feet
never
this is not your work
jesus
you have a following
people respect you
you are looked upon
  as a leader
looking into jesus' eyes
i could tell
he was serious
about washing my feet
he looked at me
smiled
lighting up
the whole room
jesus
grabbed hold of my feet

placing them
in the basin
feeling
warm water
cleaning
caked-on dirt
what was happening?
here
the one i respect
more than any other
is washing my feet
now with his hands
loosening dirt
splashing warm water
an immense joy
spread
throughout my being
jesus
i know
i want to be like you
more than anything else
in the world
to be like you
i never
thought i would be asking
you
to also let me
stoop down
take off my garments
wash the feet
of the poorest
among us

to be like you
i know
i will never forget
this moment
of feeling you clean
my feet
and doing it
with such love
to do the same
i also want to learn
to wash feet
to be a footwasher
not to seek after
the delusion of fame
of glory
to learn
every day to stoop down
to do this simple task
will put
me in touch
with you
and what you
also deeply desire
for us
to be footwashers
to wash others' feet
to be at the bottom
not to seek
to be at the top
to be a footwasher
thank you jesus
for this example

reflection questions

1. Can I let Jesus wash my feet? What did I feel as I read of Jesus' hands washing Simon Peter's feet, "loosening dirt, splashing warm water"?

2. Whose feet do I wash? In what ways do I wash their feet?

3. Do I allow others to wash my feet? In what ways does that happen?

palms

mark 11:1–11

We were preparing for Holy Week upstairs in the stuffy room of the detention unit. We divided the twelve youth into two groups. One group would plan for Palm Sunday; the other for Good Friday. Four young men were seated in a circle. As we began the reflection, I was wondering how they were ever going to relate their lives to the message of Jesus entering into Jerusalem. What happened during that hour has stayed with me. I had never understood the meaning of Palm Sunday like I did after listening to their reflections. They spoke of how afraid Jesus was to enter the city and then talked of their own fear of facing trial, of confronting an unknown and powerful system.

The first three spoke of how afraid Jesus must have been, realizing on some level that he was in for big trouble. These three minors, two of whom were facing life without parole, realized the same thing. Jesus' fear touched on their own reality: that they might never eat a meal at home again. Their fear was palpable. A heaviness came over the room. They would all be going to court the next week; no deals were being offered.

On some level Jesus knew. The fear present for these young men was the same; they knew. This feeling has stayed with me. As I celebrated Palm Sunday, I tried to feel this fear that Jesus must have had. How important

it is to overcome the fear that paralyzes us, that would
keep us from entering the city. And how important it is
to overcome this fear that would keep these young men
from sharing what they were feeling.

*When they drew near to Jerusalem and arrived at Beth-
phage and Bethany, at the Mount of Olives, Jesus sent
two of his disciples with these instructions, "Go to the
village on the other side and, as you enter it, you will find
a colt tied up that no one has ridden. Untie it and bring
it here. If anyone says to you: 'What are you doing?' give
this answer: 'The Lord needs it, but he will send it back
immediately.' "*

*They went off and found the colt out in the street tied
at the door. As they were untying it, some of the by-
standers asked, "Why are you untying that colt?" They
answered as Jesus had told them, and the people allowed
them to continue.*

*They brought the colt to Jesus, threw their cloaks on its
back, and Jesus sat upon it. Many people also spread their
cloaks on the road, while others spread leafy branches
from the fields. Then the people who walked ahead and
those who followed behind Jesus began to shout, "Hosannah! Blessed is he who comes in the name of the Lord!
Blessed is the kingdom of our father David which comes!
Hosannah in the highest!"*

*So Jesus entered Jerusalem and went into the Temple.
And after he had looked all around, as it was already late,
he went out to Bethany with the Twelve.*

> when i was small
> i used to walk
> to the synagogue
> with friends
> on the way back

i would bring
some palm branches
to my mother
the rabbi explained to us
the connection between palm branches
and our great king solomon
his vast military exploits
the pride of the people
seeing their king
entering jerusalem
on a huge stallion
the streets covered
with palm branches
these branches signifying victory
   power
   conquest
the rabbi talked of how
he yearned for those days again
i never forgot
the palm branches
i would collect
on the way back
from the synagogue
never forgot the stories
the rabbi told us
about the magnificence
of solomon
his gold his thousand troops
the power the glory the fame
as i mounted this donkey
there was a part of me
feeling how i had been

a failure
how different was my entrance
to this city of power
   of business
   of religious prestige
i looked ahead
i saw the crowds
laying palms on the road
waving them high
and further ahead the temple
   gleaming in the sun
   symbol of total power
i looked
at the faces of the campesinos
waving wildly the palms
recognized
many of them
from the furthest parts
   of the province
these folks
had come to this city of david
to spend their savings
they had earned during the year
mothers with children
   with dull looks
   from not having enough to eat
saw old men
   wrinkled weathered skin
saw young men and women
   already their faces
   aged from hard work
   hardships

as i passed
saw some whom
i had cured
of horrible skin diseases
there were no fine linen robes
lining this road
to the gates
of jerusalem
my heart pounded
seeing the gates
of the powerful
seeing the faces
   feeling the suffering
   cries of the crowd
my heart was moved
i felt connected to these faces
i wanted to offer them more
i wanted to tell them
that on one level
i would have wanted
to enter these gates
on a glorious horse
proclaiming power glory fame
i wanted to tell them
that is not my way
not from what i have learned
from my abba
my way is different
i wanted to say so much
to them as i moved
about to enter
the city that killed

her prophets
my heart was moved
feeling the pain
of these campesinos
remembering
back to the days
when the tempter
tried so hard
to convince me
into thinking
that solomon's way
was my way
was the way of my abba
i rejected
that temptation
i would not be entering
jerusalem like that
if i had chosen
wealth honor and fame
i knew that way
would not lead the people
to real liberation
   change
   equality
feeling the mystery
of self-giving love
how different
from the world's way
passing the crowds
seeing my mother
looked into her eyes
she told me long ago

that the palm branches signifying
the victory of solomon
into jerusalem
would be very different
from mine
there was a look
in her eyes
i never forgot that
and this afternoon
glancing
at my mother
i see the very same look
i wanted to yell
louder than the jubilant cries
of the crowd
why abba
this way?
why?
wanted to reach over
and ask my mother
why?
it helped looking at her
gave me strength
to draw closer
to those gates
   forbidding
   encasing such arrogant power
soon leaving behind
so many i felt connected with
who suffered so intensely
slowing passing through the gates
of jerusalem

yes mother
these palms mean something
very different
from what
they did for solomon
i am scared
entering this center of power
  very blind
  to who yahweh is
know in my heart
mother
that now it is my turn
like once
it was the turn of solomon
i come with no power
  only love
  no army
  only love
  no riches
  only love
mother
thank you
for many years ago
teaching me
that palm branches
will one day
be connected to love
  not power
  to love
  not violence
  to love
  not dominance

thank you
for teaching me
and walking with me now
to the temple
to do what i must do
to be faithful
to my abba
to those who suffer
so much from the oppression
   of the powerful
be with me
i am ready
   to be a servant
   to be a friend
   of the marginated
be with me
in dark moments ahead
in confronting the oppressors
thank you for the palm branches
   held
   in the hands
   of the poor
   from so many provinces
   who have lived
      so long
   being stepped upon
   by the strong
thank you
for showing me
a different way
   a servant
   a friend

about love
   not power
thank you mother
   now walk with me
this way sometimes
   is lonely
be with me

reflection questions

1. How did I feel when Jesus' eyes met those of his mother? What did I imagine she looked like? What did I imagine she was feeling?

2. Did anyone teach me to "be connected to love, not power; to love not violence; to love not dominance"? Who was that?

3. Does anyone walk with me when I am scared?

trial

mark 15:1-5

The courtroom in Norwalk seemed to me darker and more oppressive than others. José, a seventeen-year-old whom I had known for months from a meditation class, was to be sentenced that day. José had been in Central Juvenile Hall for a long time. He had been accused of shooting his best friend in the head. I still remember one time after a meditation, José talked about how he saw his friend in the meditation crying tears of blood. During his trial, he explained that what had happened was an accident. There was a tremendous amount of discretion in the amount of time that the judge could give in this case.

Now after months and months of court, it was time for the sentencing. Camilla, his mother, had told me before we went into the courtroom that there had been a deal worked out. It looked like they were going to give him eighteen years. For some reason, the judge was in a bad mood that day. You could sense this from the first moment he appeared. Now it was José's turn to stand before him.

The judge handed him the severest sentence possible: thirty-nine years. This was bad enough. But then he turned around and started talking to Camilla, "Where were you during those years? What kind of mother have you been?" These were the cruelest, most arrogant words I had ever heard in a courtroom. When he finished, he turned to José's godfather, Albert, and said, "And you? Where were you when José was having such problems?" I wanted to stand up and tell this judge, "How *dare* you! If you only knew how many times Camilla had tried and had sought out professional people to find some kind of help for José. Nothing ever seemed to work! No one could blame her for not being there, because she *was* there."

This judgmental condemnation really hurt. The judge gave out two life sentences that afternoon, one to José and the other to his mother. If that judge only knew what he had done that afternoon to both of them. What hope do they have, now? I thought to myself, "Someday, this judge will have to stand before another Judge."

Early in the morning, the chief priests, the elders, and the teachers of the Law (that is, the whole Council or Sanhedrin), had their plan ready. They put Jesus in chains, led him away, and handed him over to Pilate.

Pilate asked him, "Are you the King of the Jews?" Jesus answered, "You say so." As the chief priests accused Jesus of many things, Pilate asked him again, "Have you no answer at all? See how many charges they bring against you." But Jesus gave no more answers, so that Pilate wondered.

> could not help myself
> need to be here
> with jesus
> on trial

i watched how
the pharisees had crowded
around pontius pilate
watched how this was all
a sham
how are you going to get
any justice in this situation?
i watched as they brought jesus
in before the whole gathering
his hands were tied
my son looked exhausted
pilate officially began the trial
felt so sad
watching my son being treated
as a criminal
after all the people
he had helped
and here today
he was treated as a criminal
i wanted to yell out
and say something
but i decided
that would only
make things worse
pilate asking what wrong
jesus had done
found myself being angry
at these words
what wrong had he done?
he has only helped people
but he did not
bow down to the religious leaders

for this reason
they wanted to kill him
get rid of him
if only i could do something
watching all this in court
i felt so powerless
a mother watching her son
being tried
and knowing
that he is innocent
but the powerful institutions
needed a victim
and they had chosen my son
what could i do?
some people got up
talked about how jesus
had broken our law
and another
that he claims to be god's son
laughter spread through the room
when this was mentioned
god's son?
they yelled
how can this be possible?
god's son?
if they only knew
what was really happening
in this room
if they only knew
the powerful
wildly screaming
that jesus is guilty

and deserves to die
he claims to be god's son
to be god's son
guilty
how can jesus be guilty
if he has only dedicated his life
to being of help to others?
now long hours
   of condemning
   of judging
how they make fun of jesus
where were all the people
he healed?
they would never allow them
in here today
sitting in that courtroom
praying for my son
as he has to endure
this humiliation
praying
that he will be able to bear
this injustice done to him
wondering what my son
was thinking in the courtroom
i know he had seen me
when he walked in
our eyes met for one instant
what was he thinking?
he looked so tired
so sick
sitting there
watching jesus being on trial

feeling the sorrow
of a mother seeing her son
being brought
before others as a criminal
i was also praying
   for other mothers
who would have to endure
this grief
of watching their sons
be accused of things
they did not do
then stand
in front of the judge
and be ridiculed
be made fun of
for who they are
i wanted these mothers
to know that i too
the mother of god
had to bear
this heart-breaking pain
i want so much
to be able to put my arm
around jesus
and tell him how much
i his mother love him
but the mighty
in this courtroom
would never let me
get close
i wanted other mothers
who will have to sit

in courtrooms
to know that i prayed for them
this day
as my son was condemned
treated as a common criminal
god's son
treated with such disdain
as if he was
the worst sinner alive
all this
because he challenged
threatened their world of privilege
the rules of this courtroom
that favor keeping
the establishment intact

i want other mothers
to know that
i prayed for them
prayed that they too
stand with their sons
in very difficult moments
i the mother
of the son of god
will be with them
giving them strength
to endure
such a difficult ordeal
as a trial
of their son
i pray for them
that they too

find the courage
to challenge the injustices
done to their sons
done in the name of justice

reflection questions

1. Have I ever been unjustly accused? What was that like? How did I feel? Did I have the power to change the accusation?

2. Have I ever wrongly accused someone? What were my feelings as I did so? After I realized I had been wrong?

3. Can I imagine the pain of Jesus' mother? Can I imagine the pain of mothers who experience their children suffering at the hands of a power over which they have no control?

simon

mark 15:21

It is February 18, 2000. I am visiting Section 4A in the Security Housing Unit in Corcoran State Prison. Here the inmates are locked in their cells for twenty-four hours a day. At 11:00 a.m. I am summoned over to one of the glass visiting stalls. Steve begins a conversation as naturally as if we had known each other for years.

His touch on reality seems somewhat shaky, but he displays signs of gratitude that someone is listening to him. He eagerly tells me of his daily routine: he rises at 6:00 a.m., reads the Bible, does his exercises, eats, listens to programs on the radio, eats again, reads, then goes to bed. He usually does not talk to anyone all day. In order to shower, he is cuffed and has three minutes under the water along with five other inmates. They are permitted this luxury every other day. This is the only time he is let out of his cell.

The phone with which I am speaking to Steve is almost useless; the static is aggressively competing with his voice. I am forced to close my other ear and pay close attention to his words. Steve speaks of how he has not had a family visit in five years. He ends the conversation by saying how he feels cut off from everyone and everything in such isolation. He asks if I can write to him once in a while. I say that I will write.

On the way they met Simon of Cyrene (the father of Alexander and Rufus), who was coming in from the country, and forced him to carry the cross of Jesus.

all my life
i had been looking for someone
who could help
change the unjust conditions
we live under
i had listened
to jesus
   as he spoke in galilee
   then talked
   spent time with him
   i could confide in him
   open up to him
wanted to come
this afternoon to jesus
to support him
angry at those
who unjustly want to kill him
jesus
hardly had any strength left
he was falling
continually now
the romans had really tortured jesus
wiping away his strength
looking at jesus
as he fell again
under the weight of the beam

hearing someone shout at me
hey you
help this weakened one
they could do this
easily
because they knew
i was one of the many poor
from the provinces
this soldier was asking me
if i would help jesus
carry his cross
i bent down
and looked at jesus
in the face
dried blood
jesus let me take
this beam
from under your arms
wet
with sweat and blood
i will carry this wood
for you
jesus looking grateful
whispering
that i should be careful
because
they might sense
i was a disciple
i helped jesus up
supporting him
until he could balance himself
then i lifted the beam

standing next to jesus
feeling
the weight of the beam
walking next to jesus
carrying the wood
listening to the noise
of the crowds
my head spun
felt the wood
cutting into my flesh
yet walking
hearing the soldiers
screaming
to go faster
looking at the faces
of the pharisees
as they laughed at jesus
felt all this cruelty
around me
at the same time
inside
something was happening
looking at the face
of jesus
as he tried
to stumble along
felt something in my heart
i had never felt before
as hard as it was
to be laughed at
to be humiliated
to be so uncomfortable physically

i felt how glad
i could do this
that in a small way
i was supporting jesus
who had done so much
for me
never in my life
had i two movements
going on at the same time
tremendous pain
and tremendous joy
good to be able
to help jesus
my heart
went out to this one
who could barely walk
his blood dripping
onto the ground
watching jesus
i wanted so much
to tell him something
but being pushed ahead

i stopped as we climbed
a small incline
jesus bent over
saying softly
simon
thank you
these words touched me deeply
jesus thanking me
for helping him

these words
this moment
changing my life
realizing what i did
affected jesus

knowing
jesus was silently inviting me
to be a disciple
and in the future
he would invite me
to carry other crosses
but in all this
he would be affected
and would be grateful
for the willingness
to carry others' burdens
in love
how in this
accompanying others
helping them carry their cross
that in the pain
   in the suffering
   something else
will be happening
a deep profound mystery
of who god is
at his depths
self-giving love
jesus was letting me feel
god deeply
as we struggled

to go a little further
up the hill
knew i never wanted to forget
this experience

reflection questions

1. Have I experienced tremendous joy and tremendous pain in the same moment? What was that time? What caused the pain? What brought the joy?

2. Does what I do make a difference to Jesus?

3. Have I ever accompanied others? Have I helped them "carry their cross?" What feelings did I have? How did the other person respond? Could I sense that "Jesus was silently inviting me to be a disciple"?

walking with

mark 23:27–28

Because of the violence of our neighborhood, we have started a program called Caminos Seguros (Safe Passage). Some of the parish staff, along with the residents of our neighborhood, take turns going out to the streets and accompanying schoolchildren to their homes. Recently there has been a lot of shooting in the neighborhood, but by putting on our green shirts and walking along the streets with the children, it seems to help maintain a certain security in the neighborhood.

One Tuesday afternoon in October I had just begun my turn to walk the neighborhood when I heard gunshots right in front of the church. I ran over to where a boy lay bleeding in front of the church steps. The schoolchildren from the grammar school were just returning from their recreation, and mothers were on their way to pick up their children. Because I was a priest, the police permitted me to come close to where Ticio lay bleeding. He kept saying over and over again, "I don't want to die, I don't want to die." The ambulance came, and all that was left of the shooting was the stained street.

These streets have seen much blood, but that particular day the color of the blood flowing from the gunshot wound in his neck was particularly strong. We were trying to provide safe passage for our schoolchildren, and

there was one of our young people with a bullet wound
in the neck. The why and how of gangs are so complex;
it is not possible to solve the problem with one sweeping
program. But our walking, our accompanying children on
our streets, is a small sign that our God is a God who
desires life not death.

A large crowd of people followed him; among them were
women beating their breast and wailing for him, but Jesus
turned to them and said, "Women of Jerusalem, do not
weep for me, weep rather for yourselves and for your
children."

> my son had always been close
> to the outcasts
> those who society had no use for
> could hear in the distance
> shouts of
> crucify him
> crucify him
> wanted on some level
> to turn back
> but the pained look in the eyes
> of two nearby lepers
> gave me strength
> to continue walking
> my two women friends
> helped me up the incline
> i felt weak
> after the terror of last night

knowing
what the soldiers
were doing to my son
but the stories
that jesus had shared
with me
during the years
gave me strength
not to run away
jesus
with great sadness
would share with me
his visits with the youth
imprisoned for just talking
and being together
in a group
how they were mistreated
in jail
now it was my son's turn
it only made sense
that he who identified
so completely with the marginated
would find their treatment
his own
slowly making our way
to the crowd
passing by large white houses
linen blown by the hot wind
everything so beautifully arranged
the families looking out
from their balconies
with such detachment

at what was happening
to my son
families of pharisees
they seemed so confident
that their privileged world
was a blessing
from yahweh
sometimes in my own life
i had wished
i could give jesus
my son
some of the advantages
of this class
but the stories
of jesus passed through
my veins
into my heart
passing all this luxury
the memories of jesus
telling me
of his walking
to the poorest houses
of spending time
talking to those families
remembering one time
after a difficult visit
he told me how
when he helped a blind man
with twelve children
to recover his sight
that in that suffering
the misery

the humble existence
of this family
he had seen the face
of his abba
jesus told me
how his heart burnt
in that moment
was caught up
in flames
this pure joy
he would never trade
for all the comforts
of the pharisees
i smiled
as i remembered
his shiny brown eyes
his weather-worn bruised hands
my son
my son
so special
how much i love him
these memories
gave me peace
realizing something else
was happening today
not visible to the eyes
only to the heart
walking along the path
closer to the crowd
they were coming our way
turning the corner
there was my son

in front of me
truly one with the lepers
with the imprisoned youth
with the blind
the oppressed
i came closer
to jesus
the soldiers moved away
i put my hand
on the bloody shoulder
of my son
my son
my hand wet with blood
blood not being shed in vain
but would give strength
        hope
to all those who follow him
who struggle
to build a better world
the blood on my hands
burned into my heart
will never forget that moment
in the midst
of this intense sorrow
as a mother
i felt a pride
for my son
only a few will understand
this intense divine feeling
not the feeling
of the mothers
on the balconies

of the large houses
we passed
but a mother
walking with her condemned
    criminal bleeding son
my son now a common criminal
i could see
clearer
with his blood
dripping from my hands
that this is really
who god is
where he can be met
in complete self-giving
in struggling
so that others can be free
strong love
for my son
burst forth my heart
i looked
into jesus' eyes
i knew
he knew
how proud
i was of him
even in this condition
i never loved
my son
more than at that moment
what a gift
to have a son
a son

who loves the poor
so much
that out of love
out of desire
to change their condition
the powerful
treat him like a criminal
like all
who struggle
to bring justice
i would with dignity
walk the rest
of this painful path
to the hill of crucifixion
with my son
i would keep my head
held high
even with
tears of intense sorrow
        intense joy
flowing down my cheeks
my son
my son
giving his life away
truly proud of my son
        my son

reflection questions

1. When have I seen another suffer? Did I see "the face of my Abba" in that place? Was I aware of God's presence amid the suffering?

2. In what ways do I walk with Jesus on the road of suffering? With whom do I walk? Is there someone who walks with me in my suffering?

3. Do I give of myself, struggle so that others might be free? How do I do that? Can I learn to do that?

beneath the cross

mark 15:40–41

It is Good Friday, 7:00 p.m. The church is dark. We stand in front of our large statue of Our Mother of Sorrows and a cross with a crown of thorns. We began the *pésame* (condolences) service, a ritual in which we can express our sorrow to our Mother for the death of her Son. The testimony of Frank is read: "Now I am incarcerated in Central Juvenile Hall in unit MN. As a kid I went through a lot of things. My mom was a gang member, and my dad was in prison. So when I was eight years old my stepdad took away my two brothers and my sister. He told my mom that he did not want me 'cause I was not his kid. When he did that, my mom did not even care 'cause she could not afford all of us. My grandma took my mom and myself into her house. At that time I had no clothes and had no food to eat. My grandma just had enough to feed herself. My mom did not care if I ate or not. She would always be with her homeboys or homegirls partying around their neighborhood. I wish that I had a family who loved, cared for, and wanted me in their lives. Now all I can say is that people should realize what they have before they lose it for good."

Patricio, who reads this testimony, talks about how our Mother still suffers today when her children are treated badly. We now meditate on Mary as she received Jesus into her arms:

> the soldier
> who gently placed jesus
> in my arms
> feeling his body in my arms
> how i had longed
> to hold jesus firmly
> during these past days
> i felt a dampness
> of so much blood
> emanating from his clothing
> jesus my son.

What was Mary feeling?

Then each person in the church writes a letter to Mary. Virginia writes: "Maria, you are our Mother. You know what I suffer. It is so hard to be a mother today in this city. Your heart was broken like mine has been, seeing my son being treated like a criminal. I feel like you understand me better than anyone else. I give you my love. I am with you tonight."

We come forward and put the letters in front of Our Mother of Sorrows. A white carnation is placed on top of the cross. With soft background music, people are invited to leave in silence through the side doors. Everyone returns to their seats, caught up in a deep mystery of a Mother's sorrow many years ago, sensing that, right now, this is connected to the deep sorrow of many of the mothers filling the church.

There were also some women watching from a distance;
among them were Mary Magdalene, Mary the mother
of James the younger and Joset and Salome. They had
followed Jesus when he was in Galilee and helped him.
There were also many others who had come up with him
to Jerusalem.

wondering
when this would ever end
or would it ever end
wanted to escape somehow
run away from this spot
felt so weak
so vulnerable
tried to utter a prayer
recite some scripture
i had learned
when i was a small girl
but nothing came to me
as i stood beneath the cross
nothing
my emotions were frozen
had gone through so much
i noticed one soldier
to my right
he was watching me
intensely
not sure why
he came over
to where i was
he said
that he had met jesus

when he cured a roman's son
he was moved
by jesus' genuineness
watching me here
beneath the cross
he could not help
but think
of his own mother
and what it would be like
for her
to have to endure this
he told me he would command
these soldiers
to stand back
so that our group
could be close
to this condemned one
his concern was real
i accepted his offer
the soldiers
the pharisees with all their finery
moved back
leaving us
at long last
close by jesus
looked at jesus' face
jesus
this will be the last time
we will be with you alive
this is not what we were expecting
you always seemed so confident
that things were going to change

that this world would be better
but once again
it is the powerful
who are winning
i feel so destroyed
i don't want
to let hate into my heart
for these soldiers
for these religious leaders

looking up at my son
feeling the suffering
but being close
having this time
was helping me
jesus
i'll be with you
to the very end
i wish i could put myself
in your place
but i can't
i would like
to hold you in my arms
and rock you
but i can't
they are slowly
torturing you
they want to
put out your light
looking at jesus' eyes
feeling something powerful
taking place

putting my hand
around jesus' bloody feet
feeling the blood wet my hand

jesus
was trying to say something
softly hearing these words
john
i will die soon
this torture will end
i want you
to take care of my mother
to take care of my mother
john tried to say something
but he could not
he just put his arms
around me
in a very loving way
letting jesus know
that his request
was taken care of

my abba is self-giving forgiving love
friends
do not let this wrong-doing
into your own hearts
do not let bitterness
into your hearts
i know what the powerful
are doing here
is hurting you very much
everything about this cross
is unjust

i know this
but i want you to go
to another level
to find god in this darkness
put your hands
around this bloody nail
feel the blood
it is difficult to forgive
i will help you with this blood
to learn to forgive
those who try to hurt you
who will hunt you down
call you criminals
this blood will give you life
do not run away from it
rather draw strength
from this moment
god is self-giving forgiving love
knew my son
was revealing who god really is
the people here
look at him
like a common criminal
there seems to be nothing
special about him
the mothers will not
let their children
draw near
jesus' family refuses
to come near
because of the shame
the humiliation of this agonizing

slow death march
of someone who they grew up with
but being close here
with you jesus
i am feeling
a presence of your abba
know that something else
is taking place
that you can even bring light out
of this darkness
even when you seem to be losing
you are able to bring life out of it
i do not know how
i do not know how
jesus
giving your life for others
so that others
might find the strength
to give away their lives
and this is connected
to who your abba is
but who would ever think
that this is how god
would be revealed
a criminal
bloody
scorned
this is everything the opposite of
who we think god is
but this is what you my son
have always taught me
that god is in places

we least expect
all this is being summed up
in this one moment
beneath the cross
the roman soldier
with his eyes lets me know
that soon our time will be over
and the crowds will move closer
with their mocking voices
jesus i will be here to the end

i am glad
i have been your mother
you have been the best son
imaginable
even though at times
i did not understand
what you were saying
or what you were doing
i see now
that your way
is god's way
very different from the ways
of the pharisees
i cannot relieve your pain
or your suffering
but jesus as you go
to your abba
hear my words
you truly have shown god's face
even here on the cross
you have redefined who god is

you have identified with people
at the bottom
you have chosen a path
that truly shows self-giving love
shows the face of your abba
looking at jesus' eyes
i knew he had
been able to hear
what i was saying
jesus
jesus
jesus softly
saying from the cross
mother
how much
how deeply i also love you
thank you
for being here
with me
i know
this is not easy for you
i love you
very much
tears streaming down from jesus' eyes
suddenly the crowds pressed near
with vengeance
my son
showing god's face of
self-giving forgiving love

reflection questions

1. "It is difficult to forgive. I will help you with the blood to learn to forgive." Is there something I need to forgive? Can I do that with Jesus' help?

2. How do I experience God's self-giving forgiving love in my own life?

3. How do I see God's self-giving forgiving love expressed in our world? Am I able to allow God's self-giving forgiving love to be expressed through me?

receiving his body

luke 23:44–49

It is Mother's Day. Ten of the two hundred minors, because they worked on the liturgy, have been allowed to have their mothers attend the liturgy. Normally the mothers have to wait in line for hours in order to spend some time with their sons or daughters. This morning is different. The mothers arrive early to the gym, where we are going to celebrate Mass. I ask the staff if we can have some chairs for these women. To no avail: the mothers have to stand along the wall. At 8:30 the minors begin to enter the gym; they glance up and see their mothers.

They have worked hard on this liturgy. It is now their turn to come forward. I invite each one of the ten to present their moms. They give their mothers homemade cards and flowers. To see a mother receiving her incarcerated son in her arms is heartbreaking. When they read the message, it does not make any difference that there are two hundred other youth staring at them, listening to their emotional outpouring. They are lost in the moment of expressing what they feel.

Moses is making his first communion today. I am his *padrino* (godfather). Moses's father is presently serving a life sentence. He has been raised by his grandmother, Shirley. Moses was almost killed a year ago. He was paralyzed, but his strong determination saved him. He has lived life quickly. Moses reads: "I don't know what to say. You have always showed me acceptance. You have never abandoned me. It must have been hard trying to raise me, but Nana, even through all the drama you were always like a mother to me. I know there are no limits to your love."

The embrace shared between his grandmother and Moses after he read this spoke eloquently of the deep maternal love Shirley has for her seventeen-going-on-forty-year-old grandchild.

It was now about noon. The sun was hidden and darkness came over the whole land until midafternoon; and at that time the curtain of the Sanctuary was torn in two. Then Jesus gave a loud cry, "Father, into your hands, I commend my spirit." And saying that, he gave up his spirit.

The captain, on seeing what had happened, acknowledged the hand of God. He said, "Surely this was an upright man." And all the people who had gathered to watch the spectacle, as soon as they saw what had happened went home beating their breasts. Only those who knew Jesus stood at a distance, especially the women who had followed him from Galilee; they witnessed all this.

> it was over
> it finally ended
> i saw as my son took
> his last breath
> at first

i felt a strong pain
shattering my heart
but at the same time
i felt relief
after witnessing so many hours
of excruciating
suffering
under those conditions
seeing my son
so full of life
and now he was dead
without breathing
through the years
of witnessing seeing countless die
stopped breathing
but now to see my son
i had never understood
this mystery
until today
experiencing the intensity of the loss
which i had never gone through
like this before
the moment froze
everything seemed to have stopped
amid this darkness
my son
dead
lifeless
memories flowed
inside me
in this instant
it was overwhelming

my son
suddenly the soldiers
shattered the moment
placing a ladder
next to the cross
i felt
that something important
mysterious
had transpired
they could never understand
what this mystery was about
i saw my son's body
as they slowly
removed the nails
from his hands
his head dangled low
his weight
was supported
by these two soldiers
who balanced themselves
on the ladder
jesus did not move
his body lay inert
in the hands of the soldiers
i heard as a group
of pharisees laughed
talking about
how this holy man
this outcast
seemed so popular
among the people
i saw as they

made their way down the hill
the crowds slowly
moved away
i could not move
my son's death had annihilated me
the soldiers untied
what was left of jesus
from the cross
my friends had stopped crying
there was a certain stillness
a tranquility
something else was happening
after those long torturous hours
of seeing
how they treated my son
with so much cruelty
now everything was over
finally jesus lay on the ground
i sat on the rock
at the base of the cross
the soldier
carefully placed jesus
in my arms
feeling his body in my arms
how had i longed
to hold jesus firmly
during these past days
i felt the dampness
of so much blood
emanating from his clothing
jesus my son
i knew that in some way

you can still hear me
my heart is shattered
i never imagined
that this would be so painful
in so many ways
jesus
when i touch your face
when i place my hands
over your heart
i can still feel
a love
so immense
burning strongly
inside you
by feeling your mutilated body
my son
i tell you
i know
that something else
is happening
i know
that this is not the end
of the story
i felt a great mystery
a depth during these last hours
that now allows me to grab
on to this hope
i trust
that the story is not over
that in some way
you have changed history
forever

nothing will be the same
ever
because of what transpired
this afternoon
by rocking your body
back and forth
just like i used to
when you were small
i feel how much
i have yearned
to be able to embrace you
during these past few days
and now i do not want to let you go
i feel a strong connection to you
talking to you
gives me strength
gives me hope
that when everything seems
to be lost
when i embrace you
that is changed

there were a few women left
wearing humble garments
they were holding linen sheets
some had water
and others towels
i could not help being moved
by this humble act of love
of care toward my son
they were willing
to run a great risk

with so much cruelty
all around us
just for helping me
during this dangerous moment
no one knew what could happen
i gazed into their eyes
when they handed me the towels
to be soaked in the water
so i could begin washing
and cleanse the wounds
inflicted upon my son
i knew that i would not be able
to do this alone
the love
the support
of these humble women
gave me strength
to slowly wash the wounds
preparing my son for his burial
the caked blood
his whole back was an open wound
when i placed the moistened towel
inside the holes
where the soldiers placed nails
his side
was torn with a spear
feeling more than ever
a profound love
toward my son
powerful
flowing from his heart
how many mothers

will endure what i am experiencing?
their hearts smashed
how many mothers
will experience
the loss of a son?
feel so much blood
from their sons
mutilated bodies
i knew i will never forget
this moment
cleansing
my son's body
i pray for all the mothers
who will endure this pain
hoping that they will also
experience that something else
will be happening
during their moment of anguish
it is hard to explain
everything seems to be so obscure
so final
so discouraging
but this complete giving of my son
from the very heart
is what life is really about
to give your life completely
this mutilated hand
is the same hand
that he put over mine
when we strolled
the streets of nazareth
and now everything is so different

the tears streaming down my face
were also tears of love
a love that cannot be destroyed
not even by the most powerful soldiers
a divine love
i sunk my head
in my son's bloody chest

jesus
my son
how much i love you
thank you
for giving your life away
so that others can have life
i pray so that
we can soon be reunited
i will always be your mother

reflection questions

1. Do I run away from being with people who are suffering greatly?

2. Who are the people in my life who have helped me during difficult times? Who has comforted me in times of death?

3. Mary's loss was excruciating but she did not give up hope. How has God been present in my life even in the moments of great loss?

encounter

john 21:24-25

The Easter Vigil. Christ is the beginning and the end. Three hundred gather in the darkness of the parking lot of the parish grammar school. During the preceding week the Christian base communities met. We prayed and talked about how concretely during this last year God had been able to bring life out of death in our community.

Esperanza reads: "In my sons and their children I saw the face of the crucified Jesus. But the day came when they changed and they stopped following behind the cars in order to sell drugs. They have left forever their guns they once so proudly carried. Now in my family, in my sons and daughters, in my grandchildren and my parish community I see the Resurrected One."

We light the Pascal candle. Lupe shares: "I have seen and have felt so strongly the suffering in our community when we have had the shootings. All of us were discouraged but since we started Caminos Seguros (Safe Passage), we feel more protected. I am able to see a change of spirit, a spirit of Life which is manifested in the faces of our community."

We begin to light the other candles. Before we process to the church, Mario reads: "In my family I have found much life. I have felt the support of my wife during difficult moments. Her words have made me reflect and have

given me motivation to change. Each time that I overcome a negative part of myself, something that does not give life to my family, I feel the presence of the Resurrected One."

It is now time for the adult baptisms. Our God is a God who can bring life out of death. As we welcome these adults into our community, we are also celebrating how our God, in this community, this year, in spite of so much darkness, continues to give life.

It is this disciple who testifies about the thing he has recorded here and we know that his testimony is true. But Jesus did many other things; if all were written down, I think that the world itself would not hold the books recording them.

> all night long
> staring out the window
> the memories of these past days
> passing through my mind
> tearing apart my heart
> especially scenes
> of how jesus
> was destroyed
> by the soldiers
> ridiculed by the pharisees
> looking out my window
> as the horizon
> was slowly lightening
> staring out the window
> so much sadness
> asking myself again
> why?
> why does it seem yahweh
> has abandoned us?
> why?

why did all this have
to happen
to my only son?
why?
staring out
at the subtle change
from total darkness
to dawning
slowly
in this instant
in which
night becomes day
i heard my name
called
ever so softly
mother
jesus
softly saying
mother
i am here
felt the sun rising
in my heart
no longer dawn
the sun strong
jesus saying
i was grateful to you mother
to all those women
who helped
wash clean prepare
my body for the burial
i was treated
like how all the poor

have been treated
for years
jesus
i want to ask
you
so many questions
what is going
to happen now?
how is the kingdom
of our abba
to be established?
i don't want
to lose you again
jesus
i have thought
during these days
of the mothers
who have to endure
what i have endured
where will they find hope?
what will they do
with the loss of their sons?
i know jesus
being here with you
at this moment
you are answering this
this love
between mothers and sons
cannot be destroyed
by roman soldiers
by the high priests
it is eternal

mother
you have seen
what happens
when the center of power
is threatened
total destruction
for anyone
who challenges
this way of life
but my rising
from the dead
mother
is a sign
that it is not in vain
to struggle
to reverse the order
of the dominant
it is not the will
of my abba
that so many have nothing
while a few have so much
during future days
mother
i will be connected
to all those
who struggle
to build a better world
mother
i could feel
your love for me
when i met you
on the way to the golgotha

my body was agonizing
in pain
i only felt darkness
but looking into your eyes
i knew you understood
the cost of giving
your life away
in the struggle
to help build
a better world
your support
i so deeply
appreciated
was important
that a few
could understand
the mystery
taking place

i thank you mother
and i thank all mothers
who will follow you
who will support
their sons
in their struggles
it will not be easy
there will be pain
anguish darkness
intense
but never
never lose hope
i have risen

i have turned
death into life
this is what
must be held on to
that i can bring
light from darkness
jesus
what you say is true
i pray
for all mothers
so that they
can experience
the hope
that i am experiencing
jesus
thank you
for visiting me
and permitting me to feel
this hope
hope in one once dead
now alive

reflection questions

1. Do I have hope? What gives me hope?

2. Do I know someone who is a hopeful person? What in that person's life expresses hope to me?

3. Where is hope needed in my life? in my community? in my city? in my world? Can I be a part of bringing the hope of the resurrection?

road

luke 24:13–28

It was 1:00 p.m. Wednesday afternoon. The day before, March 7, was election day. For many months our church had worked hard to defeat Proposition 21, which would try youth in the adult system with much more frequency. Basically, this proposition would undermine the juvenile system in this state. The proposition passed overwhelmingly. That Wednesday it was difficult not to feel angry, frustrated, and disappointed by the results. The hours and hours of working, walking precincts, phone calls, press conferences, vigils, all seemed to have been to no avail. It was now time for an afternoon meditation in the church. We used the passage about the disciples on the road to Emmaus, when they left Jerusalem after they had seen Jesus die on the cross.

After the meditation, Martín spoke. I had gotten to know Martín and his wife, Letty, through his son Carlos, whom I knew during his stay at Juvenile Hall. Carlos is now in prison serving eleven years. When Martín spoke that afternoon, after this terrible defeat, he expressed the same hope that I have heard from him before. It is the same hope that he discovered in visiting and keeping alive his relationship with his son. When he spoke that afternoon, I knew that what he said about hope was true because of the transformation I have seen take place in him. This hope is so strong now that every week Martín and his wife go to Juvenile Hall to visit the minors. He also reaches out to many of the parents whose sons are incarcerated.

At one time, it seemed everything was over for Martín and Letty, having a son locked up for so many years. It was just like when the disciples left Jerusalem and headed toward Emmaus; Jesus was dead and everything was over. Everything seemed dark and defeated that Wednesday in the church, but Martín was able to speak about the same hope that grew in the hearts of the disciples walking with this Stranger. He spoke of how it had not been in vain, all the effort, all the night meetings, all the work done during those long months of effort to defeat this proposition. Now more than ever we needed to be united to work for the youth of our community.

Slowly, a different feeling could be felt in the church. Slowly, others began to speak about how they wished to continue to meet together and to see what they could do to change unjust laws. Hearts were burning with renewed hope.

Martín extended an invitation to the group to accompany him to Juvenile Hall the following Sunday. When they arrived, this small group of faithful workers were called up in front in the gym in front of three hundred minors. They were presented with flowers and a certificate of appreciation for all their work in trying to defeat Proposition 21. Martín talked about how he realized that this was not the end. There was still much to do for the youth of our community. We experienced defeat and felt discouraged. But we also knew hope through our work and prayer together, a hope that is deeper and more powerful than our discouragement. We will continue our efforts.

That same day, two of them were going to Emmaus, a village seven miles from Jerusalem, and they talked about what had happened. While they were talking and wondering, Jesus came up and walked with them, but their eyes were held and they did not recognize him.

He asked, "What is this you are talking about?" The two stood still, looking sad. Then one named Cleophas answered, "Why, it seems you are the only one in Jerusalem who doesn't know what has happened there these past few days." And he asked, "What is it?"

They replied, "It is about Jesus of Nazareth. He was a prophet, you know, mighty in word and deed before God and the people. But the chief priests and our rulers sentenced him to death. They handed him over and he was crucified. Yet we had hoped that he would redeem Israel.

"It is now the third day since all this took place. What amazes us greatly is the strange tale some of our women pass around. They went to the tomb early this morning, but didn't find his body. When they came back to us, they had a story about seeing a vision of angels who told them that Jesus was alive. Some friends of our group went to the tomb and found everything just as the women said, but him they did not see."

He said to them, "How dull you are, how slow of understanding! You fail to believe the message of the prophets. Is it not written that the Christ should suffer all this and then enter his glory?" Then starting with Moses and going through the prophets, he explained to them everything in Scripture concerning himself.

As they drew near the village they were heading for, Jesus made as if to go farther.

> walking through tall gates
> whitened by the burning sun
> walking through these gates
> wanted to leave behind the pain
> of past days
> walking slowly
> talking with my friend
> walking
> reflecting
> going over the details
> of jesus' death
> the pace was slow
> in comparison
> to other days
> today we are not racing
> trying to do many things
> didn't make any difference
> everything was over
> this one who was executed
> was the one
> who taught us how to walk
> with others
> walking this day to emmaus
> having time on this journey
> to stop
> and talk with other travelers

about what had happened
in jerusalem
there was time
to breathe in the countryside
even though our world had ended
even though life seemed
to be different
without meaning
there was time now
walking slowly
accompanying
a cripple to his house
accompanying
an elderly woman
to her next stop
there was time
to walk
without running
without being distracted
able to be present
to each person
we encountered
all this
we had learned
from walking with the master
soon we were far
from jerusalem
journeying
with our slow pace
it was easy
to have a fast-paced traveler
suddenly catch up with us

now there were three walking
the way
he walked reminded me
of how the master
walked
he paid attention
to what
we were saying
like jesus had done
what we said
mattered to him
could not believe
he did not seem to know
how they killed the nazarean
he asked us questions
as the three of us
walking
sometimes
we stopped
and sat under the shade
of protecting trees
there was also time
for this
walking with this stranger
was like
walking with jesus
there was time to engage
enjoy the moment
not being controlled
by everyone's demands
by false pressures
by too much work

walking with this traveler
i began to ask him
the questions
that had been going around
within me
for days
he seemed
to have studied well the torah
he seemed to have a wisdom
after talking for hours
taking our time
walking
i asked him
why did all the events
of the past days
have to happen?
why did yahweh
allow this to happen?
why?
i did not want to blaspheme
against the holy one
but why?
this stranger
listened to me
and smiled
why?
friend
you wanted yahweh
to intervene
to have stopped the cruelty
done to his anointed one
so he would not have to suffer

why did he have to suffer
so much?
why?
we stopped
the stranger wrote on the ground
the names of the holy men and women
who were part
of our history
was even one of these
spared
from so much suffering?
they spoke the truth
to the powerful
the consequences followed
that is the way
of the prophet
of the one
who speaks the truth
it is not
an easy way
we sat for a long time
as this one
explained about the way
of the prophets
how nowhere
in our scripture
does it say
we will not have to suffer
but rather suffering
can be transformed
why didn't yahweh
rescue jesus?

because as the anointed one
he showed us
he is one
connected
with all those
who struggle
he was not singled out
and spared
the consequences
but experienced
the same plight of others
before him who had been executed
rather he has brought
transforming meaning
in his death
slowly
as slowly
as our pace
i began to see
began to understand
like i never have been
able to understand before
the way of yahweh
that the prophets' way
is not to escape suffering
run away from it
but for his reign
to embrace it
and then something will happen
maybe not right away
it will not be easy
but something more

will be happening
when we walk
the way of the prophets
the question of why
will be answered
in the walking with
no easy answers
will be given
but the very act
of accompanying
of walking with
entering into the struggle
will provide you
with the understanding
   the answer
could now see
knew by running away
   from jerusalem
   was not the answer
rather i knew
in that moment
walking with this stranger
that i would need
to journey back to the place
that was responsible
for executing jesus
was so moved
by the words
of this stranger
that my heart raced faster
without having to give
a specific answer

he was giving me
meaning
explaining yahweh's way
understanding
that i would be thrown out
of the temple
if i returned
to jerusalem
glad
for this time
walking
with this stranger
walking
sharing
so that when i returned
and confronted the religious leaders
how they were treating
the people
with such heavy taxes
i would be living the answer
  to my question
  of why the master
  was put to death
knew
when i returned
and brought my friend the leper
food
against all the laws
of our country
and could not return
to where i live
i would be living

the answer to my question
hope burning bright within
as this one walked with us
slowly walking
let me see
that the answer
to the why of suffering
is found in the walking with
accompanying
those who have been left out
by society
to walk this path
of the prophets
feeling heart burning
giving me strong desire
to return to this struggle
heart in flames

reflection questions

1. Is there time in my life for walking with the stranger I meet along the road? Could I make time?

2. "The prophets' way is not to escape suffering, run away from it, but...to embrace it and then something will happen." Have I seen suffering embraced by a person? a community? Did something happen? Have I experienced that in my own life?

3. How am I being asked to embrace suffering in my life now? Can I embrace the suffering and have faith that something will happen?

Just mercy.
- movie -

sp?

Philakoloba.